The God 2 Know

The God I Know

DEMARIO L. ROLLINS

XULON PRESS

Xulon Press
2301 Lucien Way #415
Maitland, FL 32751
407.339.4217
www.xulonpress.com

Xulon PRESS

© 2021 by Demario L. Rollins

All rights reserved solely by the author. The author guarantees all contents are original and do not infringe upon the legal rights of any other person or work. No part of this book may be reproduced in any form without the permission of the author. The views expressed in this book are not necessarily those of the publisher.

Due to the changing nature of the Internet, if there are any web addresses, links, or URLs included in this manuscript, these may have been altered and may no longer be accessible. The views and opinions shared in this book belong solely to the author and do not necessarily reflect those of the publisher. The publisher therefore disclaims responsibility for the views or opinions expressed within the work.

Unless otherwise indicated, Scripture quotations taken from the Amplified Bible (AMP). Copyright © 1954, 1958, 1962, 1964, 1965, 1987 by The Lockman Foundation. Used by permission. All rights reserved.

Scripture quotations marked EHV are from the Holy Bible, Evangelical Heritage Version® (EHV®) © 2019 Wartburg Project, Inc. All rights reserved. Used by permission.

Scripture quotations from The New Testament for Everyone are copyright © Nicholas Thomas Wright 2011.

Scripture quotations taken from the American Standard Version (ASV)) – public domain

Scripture quotations taken from the Common English Bible® (CEB) Copyright © 2010, 2011 by Common English Bible.™ Used by permission. All rights reserved worldwide.

Scripture quotations taken from the Contemporary English Version (CEV). Copyright © 1995 American Bible Society. Used by permission. All rights reserved.

Scripture quotations taken from the Complete Jewish Bible (CJB). Copyright © 1998 by David H. Stern. All rights reserved. No portion of this book may be reproduced, stored in a retrieval system, or transmitted in any form or by any means without prior written permission of the publisher.

Scripture quotations taken from the Christian Standard Bible. (CSB). Copyright © 2017 by Holman Bible Publishers. Used by permission. All rights reserved.

Scripture quotations taken from the The Easy-to-Read Version (ERV). Copyright © 2006 by Bible League international.

Scripture taken from The Expanded Bible (TEV). Copyright ©2011 by Thomas Nelson. Used by permission. All rights reserved.

Scripture quotations taken from the English Standard Version (ESV). Copyright © 2001 by Crossway, a publishing ministry of Good News Publishers. Used by permission. All rights reserved.

Scripture quotations taken from the Gods Word Translation copyright ©1995 by Baker Publishing Group.

Scripture quotations taken from the Good News Translation (GNT). Copyright © 1992 American Bible Society. Used by permission. All rights reserved.

Scripture quotations taken from the Holman Christian Standard Bible (HCSB). Copyright © 1999, 2000, 2002, 2003, 2009 by Holman Bible Publishers, Nashville Tennessee. All rights reserved.

Scripture quotations taken from the International Children's Bible (ICB). The Holy Bible, International Children's Bible® Copyright© 1986, 1988, 1999, 2015 by Tommy Nelson™, a division of Thomas Nelson. Used by permission.

Scripture quotations taken from The Holy Bible: International Standard Version. Release 2.0, Build 2015.02.09. Copyright © 1995-2014 by ISV Foundation. ALL RIGHTS RESERVED INTERNATIONALLY. Used by permission of Davidson Press, LLC.

Scripture quotations taken from the King James Version (KJV) – public domain.

Scripture quotations marked (LEB) are from the Lexham English Bible. Copyright 2012 Logos Bible Software. Lexham is a registered trademark of Logos Bible Software.

Scripture quotations taken from the Living Bible (TLB). Copyright © 1971 by Tyndale House Foundation. Used by permission of Tyndale House Publishers Inc., Carol Stream, Illinois 60188. All rights reserved.

Scripture quotations taken from The Message (MSG). Copyright © 1993, 1994, 1995, 1996, 2000, 2001, 2002. Used by permission of NavPress Publishing Group. Used by permission. All rights reserved.

Scripture quotations taken from the Scripture is taken from GOD'S WORD® (NOG), © 1995 God's Word to the Nations. Used by permission of Baker Publishing Group.

Scripture quotations taken from the New American Standard Bible (NASB). Copyright © 1960, 1962, 1963, 1968, 1971, 1972, 1973, 1975, 1977, 1995 by The Lockman Foundation. Used by permission. All rights reserved.

Scripture quotations taken from New Life Version (NLV). Copyright © 1969 by Christian Literature International.

Scripture quotations taken from the New Century Version (NCV). Copyright © 2005 by Thomas Nelson, Inc. Used by permission. All rights reserved.

Scripture quotations taken from the New English Translation (NET Bible). Copyright ©1996-2006 by Biblical Studies Press, L.L.C. Used by permission. All rights reserved.

Scripture quotations taken from the New King James Version (NKJV). Copyright © 1982 by Thomas Nelson, Inc. Used by permission. All rights reserved.

Scripture quotations taken from New International Reader's Version (NIRV). Copyright © 1995, 1996, 1998, 2014 by Biblica, Inc.®. Used by permission. All rights reserved worldwide.

Scripture quotations taken from the Holy Bible, New Living Translation (NLT). Copyright ©1996, 2004, 2007 by Tyndale House Foundation. Used by permission of Tyndale House Publishers, Inc.

Scripture quotations taken from the New Revised Standard Version (NRSV). Copyright © 1989 the Division of Christian Education of the National Council of the Churches of Christ in the United States of America.

Scripture quotations taken from the Holy Bible, New International Version (NIV). Copyright © 1973, 1978, 1984, 2011 by Biblica, Inc.™. Used by permission. All rights reserved.

Scripture quotations taken from the Revised Standard Version (RSV). Copyright © 1946, 1952, and 1971 the Division of Christian Education of the National Council of the Churches of Christ in the United States of America. Used by permission. All rights reserved.

Scripture quotations are taken from the JB Phillips (PHILLIPS), by J. B. Phillips, "The New Testament in Modern English", Copyright© 1962 edition, published by HarperCollins. Used by permission. All rights reserved.

Scripture taken from The Passion Translation (TPT). Copyright © 2017 by Passion & Fire Ministries, Inc. Used by permission. All rights reserved. thePassionTranslation.com

Tree of Life (TLV) Translation of the Bible. Copyright © 2015 by The Messianic Jewish Family Bible Society.

Scripture quotations taken from the Word English Bible (WEB)–*public domain.*Printed in the United States of America.

ISBN-13: 978-1-6628-1344-3
Ebook 978-1-6628-1345-0

Dedications

To the **Author of Life** itself, You gave it ALL for me. If I could but grant a moment of this life to offer you mine in its total essence without flaw, that I would do, not for a moment but for all eternity. Instead, I defer completely to Your saving grace, for within this frame of human frailty bears no ounce or fragment of perfection apart from the presence of Your indwelling Spirit. I submit my life as an offering poured out in a sweet discord of broken melodies. Though applause may come from those who observe or benefit from this *imperfect rhapsody* (***my life***), I long evermore to see You rise from the balcony in satisfaction with the life I've offered. Not of my own accord, but all this is from You, who reconciled me to You through Christ Jesus (2 Corinthians 5:18). Did I tell You I love You today? Did I tell You I miss You today? Did I tell You "thank You" today? Did I tell You that I "just want to be with You?" The end I seek is to give You all of me. It is the only reasonable response to the *ineffable sacrifice* You willingly gave on the cross (***Your life***). The relationship I desire is that of true love and allegiance to You; You are Love. The life I live is to become the best worshipper of You in this phase of existence as I ever hope to be in the phase called next, for eternity has already begun.

To my *cherished* **Flower**, when God chose to coalesce our paths, He gave me a priceless treasure. My life more adequately and appropriately resembles the Son because of your love, patience, and encouragement. Words cannot express the sincere appreciation I have for you and your impact on the trajectory of my life. I'm a better man, husband, dad, pharmacist, author, teacher, and preacher because of your faithfulness to our Savior. You are my final destination before Heaven. I look forward to changing the world with you. We will absolutely leave it better than we found it! God chose an exceptional steward for my heart. *Find a good spouse, you find a good life— and even more: the favor of God!* (Proverbs 18:22 The Message).

To my *sweet* **Makayela**, you bring energy and excitement to every human who has the privilege of being in your presence. Thank you for making us proud as you mature into the young adult Jesus always had in mind. Whatever path you choose to take, your courage and perseverance will pave the way to your success. His goodness and mercy will follow you all the days of your life (Psalm 23:6).

To my *darling* **Maddie**, you epitomize empathy and naturally gravitate toward the temperature of those in your atmosphere. Your warmth in times of cheer and comfort in times of gloom demonstrate the

Dedications

compassion of Jesus in a unique way. You look for the good in others and encourage them with kind words. I can always count on you to evoke a smile secondary to your words of kindness and affirmation.

To my *dearest* **Micah**, you are a joy to be around and a delight to have around. Your firm hugs, hearty laughter, and random "I love you's" make for great days at home. Thank you for completing our 5-pack in superb style. I've seen and heard you do more spiritual things than some people four times your age and I can't wait to see what God is going to do through you!

To my *respected* **Dad,** you are a very special person. Sometimes I look in the mirror and instead of seeing myself...I see you. It's interesting how much I'm beginning to favor you as I age. (Makayela often says certain expressions I make remind her of you). I'm proud to "look like you" because it reminds me that I am the child of a man that I'm very proud of. I'm proud of your decision to follow Jesus. I'm proud of your career as a mechanic. I'm proud of the integrity and responsibility you instilled in me. I'm proud of the support you've given me over the years. I'm proud to be your son. Thank you for being my dad!

To my *loving* **Brother**, what can I say? You're simply the best brother one could have. You love Jesus more than life itself. You inspired me to race bikes when I was only four years old! You demonstrated the art of humor with such finesse that it motivated me to embark upon my own version of comicality. I have years of loving memories of a brother who NEVER lets me forget how much I'm dearly loved by him. Thank you for being my brother and demonstrating Jesus' love by loving me unconditionally!

To my *virtuous* **Mother**, thank you for being my biggest cheerleader! Through it all, you have been a source of wisdom and grace. I am many miles from perfect, but in my pursuit of it, I have tried my very best to make you proud and bring honor to you in the process. Thank you for introducing me to Jesus Christ! You filled my heart with His Word before I took my first breath outside of my 9 month apartment. Thank you for praying for me incessantly!

To my *honored* **Reader**, I pray that the pages you are about to read will intrigue and captivate you beyond your unexpected expectations. May you laugh, cry, pray, sing, dance, forgive, and seek the face and heart of the THE ONE who created yours.

Contents

Chapter 1:. Relationships. 1
"Try to enjoy every day with your significant other as if it's the last. Tomorrow isn't promised to any of us. All that we have today could be gone tomorrow, including our lives. Think before you speak, say only what you wouldn't mind being repeated on the loudspeaker at a Major League Baseball game. Smile, laugh, and savor special moments. Carve special memories in stone and remember them forever. Write your hurts on the seaside so that the tide will wash their memory away."

Chapter 2:. Progeny 13
Children are an inheritance from the Lord. They are a reward from him. The children born to a man when he is young are like arrows in the hand of a warrior. Blessed is the man who has filled his quiver with them. He will not be put to shame when he speaks with his enemies in the city gate. (Psalm 127:3-5 GW).

Chapter 3:. Depression **23**
"It is so sad but I only know where I have been and where I am. I have no idea where I am going or for the matter of it…where I want to go. I have no hopes, I have no dreams, and I have no meaning that I am aware of. This is my loneliness and this is my depression."

Chapter 4:. Loneliness **37**
"It is sad but perhaps true that the rejection I have received throughout the course of my life has played an *instrumental* role in the *song of dismay* my life is now *recording.*"

Chapter 5:. Purpose **43**
"My purpose is to encourage, inspire, and instruct others to understand, appreciate, and express the love given to us by the Father through the sacrifice of Jesus Christ by first inspiring them to have hope through laughter, joy, and forgiveness but ultimately by accepting Jesus Christ as Lord and Savior by the empowerment of the Holy Spirit."

Chapter 6:. Salvation **65**
"I won't be beneficial to you in spiritual matters unless you decide that you are separated from God due to sin and that the only way back to Him is through Jesus Christ."

Chapter 7:. Service **77**

Dedications

"Learn to give more and more of your daily cares to the One who cares daily for you."

Chapter 8:. Worship 85

"At the heart of worship is the heart of the worshipper. A heart surrendered is a heart that is thankful. A heart that is thankful is a heart that seeks to adore the One responsible for its existence."

Chapter 9:. Marriage 91

"To make marriage work you MUST take the exit door off its hinges and erect a brick wall 54 feet deep in its place that can NEVER be penetrated. Marriage requires audacious commitment and the relentless courage to be *willingly*, *sacrificially*, and safely *sequestered* in this once in a lifetime opportunity."

Chapter 10:. Discipleship 111

"As humans, we are bent toward forgetting unless we are intentional."

— Heather D. Rollins

Preface:

> "If but one soul may declare after mine has departed, that the life I lived in some way, form, or fashion was a display of my invisibility and Christ's visibility through my existence, then the purpose for which I was created was not vanity." —Demario L. Rollins

The Trinity is incomprehensibly the most ineffable mystery one shall ever attempt to comprehend. There are many books that could be written and indeed have been written concerning the Most High. The chapters and contents that shall ensue may seem to embark upon a topic of interest without fulfilling a substantial portion of the subject itself, only to culminate prematurely without adequate closure. This is intentional. Somewhere in the **abridge***ment,* I pray that you will find in Him **a bridge** *meant* for you to traverse every obstacle impeding your progress.

Introduction:

> "Each day I am permitted to breathe, every decision I make, every word I speak, every action performed, every forgiveness granted, and every passing thought is filtered with and through this one question...How do I want to be remembered?"—Demario L. Rollins

It was a cold New Years night when I found myself kneeling in my closet with tears running down my face. No interruptions, no appointments, no text messages, no distractions, just God and me. Surrounded by clothes, shoes, posted prayers on walls, and my favorite poster containing 54 names of my Savior, I mentally navigated through the unexplainable sacrifice made by Jesus to leave Heaven and trade it for me.

Early the next morning before the first spray of sunlight misted the crisp frozen Arkansan dew, I knew it was time to begin, "The God I Know". Inspiration place, yes, you guessed it, the *restroom*. The room within the home I freely disclose, the specific manner in which I chose to *rest* shall remain enigmatic. Does anyone else get inspired while resting in that room? Intrinsic responses recommended.

Chapter 1: Relationships

> "Try to enjoy every day with your significant other as if it's the last. Tomorrow isn't promised to any of us. All that we have today could be gone tomorrow, including our lives. Think before you speak, say only what you wouldn't mind being repeated on the loudspeaker at a Major League Baseball game. Smile, laugh, and savor special moments. Carve special memories in stone and remember them forever. Write your hurts on the seaside so that the tide will wash their memory away."

It was winter 2018 and there I stood at the register, helping yet another customer in one of the busiest and active flu seasons I've experienced as a Pharmacist. I exaggerate not when I tell you that kindness was not a prerequisite to visit our medicine shop that day. Not many of our valued guests offered positive words or delightful gestures. Nevertheless, I brought my own joy to work with me and did not permit my outward circumstances to infiltrate the fun-filled carnival going on internally. One of the customers who witnessed my unfortunate encounters with the mean-spirited public and the overwhelming circumstances under which we were working complimented me on the way I was handling the situation. I told her that I was able to smile, laugh, and keep a positive attitude because of Jesus. I said, "the first and greatest commandment is to love God with all of my heart, soul, mind, and strength and the second is to love you as I love myself" (Mark 12:30-31). By the look on her face you would have thought I had a seven-headed giraffe growing out of my nose. She said, "If only we all thought and behaved that way, we need more people like you in this world." To which I replied, "That's what He said in the Bible and that's what I should be doing." But, to myself, I'm thinking…"*That's what we all should be doing*!" If we call ourselves Christians, shouldn't we follow Christ? Jesus said the world would know us by our love (John 13:35). So, shouldn't we love one another as He loves us and as we love ourselves? I submit to you that many travelers in this foreign land called Earth have forgotten that we only have one enemy, the Devil. We omit to remember that we were all made in God's image and in His own likeness. As John would later say after Jesus' ascension,

Chapter 1: Relationships

"If we don't love people we can see, how can we love God, whom we cannot see?" (I John 4:20b NLT).

As I observe those around me and the manner in which they respond to others, the primary ingredient absent in their assessment and reactions is undoubtedly unconditional love. In some cases, it is simply a lack of love altogether. The Bible says we should be quick to listen, slow to speak and slow to become angry (James 1:19). We are also encouraged, as far as it depends on us, to live at peace with everyone (Romans 12:18). Without love, we automatically react to the situation at hand with a type of auto-response based on our life experiences and how they have shaped us. Though we may become angry, we can do so without sinning (Ephesians 4:26). If we could but be still and know that He is God (Psalm 46:10), then, **in that moment** the Advocate, the Holy Spirit will remind us of everything the Lord has said (John 14:26). He will use the scriptures that we daily feed upon to remind us of the truth. We are, in that moment, face to face with a creation that was fearfully and wonderfully made in the image of the Most High God. What a marvelous thought! Is it not astonishing that every human being bears a family resemblance of the One who exchanged His righteousness for our filth?

In the sermon on the mount, Jesus said, *"Blessed are you when men hate you, and when they exclude and mock you, and throw out your name as evil, for the Son of Man's sake. Rejoice in that day, and leap for joy, for behold, your reward is great in heaven, for their fathers did the same thing to the prophets."* (Luke 6:22-23 WEB).

Could difficult people be a test?

Could persecution or perceived persecution be an opportunity to fulfill scripture?

Could our response to challenging circumstances be a light to a dark world?

One of my favorite scriptures in all of the Bible is found in Philippians. *Do not be concerned about your own interests, but also be concerned about the interests of others.* (Philippians 2:4 ISV). I love people! I genuinely love people! Yes, they can be abrupt, obnoxious, rude, unfair, hateful, selfish, mean, and unforgiving. But, through the eyes of Jesus, I see a soul that He decided to create as a part of His story. That soul deserves to know about Heaven and Hell. That soul deserves to experience only one of those destinations through my interactions with them. I cannot say it better than the Holy Spirit did through Peter, *"Above all, maintain an intense love for each other, since love covers a multitude of sins"* (1 Peter 4:8 HCSB).

Having been diagnosed with dysfluency at age 4, undergoing speech therapy through Easter Seals, and struggling to put sentences together, I have acquired a fair appreciation for communication and the words that are utilized to construct the exchange of thought. Subsequently, my youngest daughter has become the proud recipient of vocabulary words such as chlorophyll,

Chapter 1: Relationships

perforation, contemplating and the recent addition of a comparison and contrast exercise. While sharing a special moment in the little room where we have the privilege to part with cellular waste, she noticed that some toilets flushed by themselves while others required effort from the user. I took this opportunity to impart knowledge to her that would hopefully get her to skip a grade in school someday. I tactfully informed her that if a toilet flushed by itself that it was "automatic" and if we had to do it, it was "manual". She seemed to enjoy this new information so I've been sure to give pop quizzes during future micturition experiences! Wouldn't it be nice if forgiveness worked like the toilets that startle us from time to time because we're not actually finished yet? Well, I've upgraded my forgiveness muscle to work in that way and I'd like to suggest that you do the same! *Your heavenly Father will forgive you if you forgive those who sin against you; but if you refuse to forgive them, he will not forgive you* (Matthew 6:14-15 TLB). Because of this truth, I have practiced forgiving those who offend me as an automatic response to their offense. As soon as the offense is over (and sometimes while it's still going on), I forgive them. In fact, since I know forgiveness is a requirement on this journey, I have written a blank check to the world's population in anticipation of both offenses and the pardon I have already decided to grant. This bold approach to relationships can ONLY be accomplished through the power of the indwelling

Holy Spirit. He is the forgiver! I am the yielder. He pardons the offense. I submit in humility and admiration of the Father's great tolerance of my own wretchedness. *A further reason for forgiveness is to keep from being outsmarted by Satan; for we know what he is trying to do.* (2 Corinthians 2:11 TLB).

In relationships it is important to maintain control of our emotions. "*Be sober, be vigilant; because your adversary the devil walks about like a roaring lion, seeking whom he may devour*" (1 Peter 5:8 NKJV). Our enemy delights in our ignorance of him and our unwarranted focus on one another. *For we wrestle not against flesh and blood, but against principalities, against powers, against the rulers of the darkness of this world, against spiritual wickedness in high places* (Ephesians 6:12 KJV).

At some point, Satan cleverly convinced us that he's not real. Furthermore, he has downgraded the value of human life and desensitized us to the practice and consequences of sin. We blame one another for our own insufficiencies and the error of our ways. Doesn't that sound familiar and tantamount to life in the Garden of Eden when Adam and Eve heard the Lord God walking in the garden after they disobeyed His command (Genesis 3:8)? Adam blamed Eve and Eve blamed the serpent. The serpent? There he is again! Lucifer, Satan, our one true enemy. *The thief comes only in order to steal, kill, and destroy* (John 10:10a GNT). However, we can be of good cheer because the

Chapter 1: Relationships

Son of God appeared to destroy the works of the Devil (1 John 3:8). We are more than conquerors through Him who loves us (Romans 8:37)! Jesus dealt a decisive blow to Satan on the cross by disarming the spiritual rulers and authorities. He shamed them publicly by his victory over them on the cross (Colossians 2:15). The victory He won "publicly" extends to those "private" moments in our mind and heart when we would otherwise respond in relationships the way we've been conditioned. Let me take this opportunity to restate what was mentioned earlier.

"Without love, we automatically react to the situation at hand with a type of auto-response based on our life experiences and how they have shaped us. Though we may become angry, we can do so without sinning (Ephesians 4:26). If we could but be still and know that He is God (Psalm 46:10), then, **in that moment** the Advocate, the Holy Spirit will remind us of everything the Lord has said (John 14:26). He will use the scriptures that we daily feed upon to remind us of the truth."

That reminds me of an interaction between Jesus and Pilate before the crucifixion:

> *Pilate asked him, "So you are a king?" Jesus answered, "You say that I am a king. For this I was born, and for this I came into the world, to testify to the truth. Everyone who belongs to the truth*

listens to my voice." Pilate asked him, "What is truth?" (John 18:37-38 NRSV).

Do you recognize the truth when you hear it? You can't know truth until you know the One who is Truth. **In that moment**, that small fraction of time, we can either *choose to yield* our response to the leadership of the Holy Spirit or *automatically react* to the situation at hand with a type of auto-response based on our life experiences and how they have shaped us. And a yet greater misfortune is to permit Satan to accomplish his wicked schemes through us. Charles R. Swindoll said that "life is 10% what happens to me and 90% how I react to it". Practicing the command to love with a tenacious effort to yield our relationships to the guidance of the Holy Spirit will ensure that the 90% that falls our way will make Jehovah smile.

A young lady whom we will call "friend" asked me, whom we will call "Demario", how he deals with negative people. Apparently, it created a mental anomaly for her to receive negativity and lack of appreciation from the very individuals she "bends over backwards" for. The following represents "Demario's" original response to "friend" with scripture references added later.
Friend: How do you deal with negative people?

Demario: When God, Jesus, and the Holy Spirit decided to make mankind they decided to make him in God's image (Genesis 1:26). Therefore, every human is an

Chapter 1: Relationships

image bearer of God. I am madly in love with God and that means that I love Him and everything that is like Him. The Bible commands us to love God with all of our heart, mind, and soul and to love our neighbor as we love ourselves. (Mark 12:29-31).

Demario: I love people, not necessarily because they deserve to be loved, but because I love God so much. (Matthew 22:37).

Demario: If you think of it, all sin and difficulties originated from Satan. He is my only one true enemy. So when a human being is being difficult, I know that it is not the human, but it is the Enemy that is working through them to try and upset me or discourage me or hurt me. (Ezekiel 28:15; 1 Peter 5:8).

Demario: He that is in me is greater than he that is in the world. When Christ died on the cross He openly defeated Satan and all of his demons. It is my choice whether I choose to allow negative people to offend or affect me. (1 John 4:4; Colossians 2:15).

Demario: I choose to live not according to what's going on around me but according to the joy that is within... given to me by my Savior Jesus Christ.

Demario: I live for Him.

Demario: No *one* else.

Demario: No *thing* else.

Demario: The Bible tells us to love our enemies. If I did not have any enemies then how could I follow the Bible's teaching by loving them? I need difficult people in my life to show them God's love and to know that I am following Him completely (Matthew 5:44).

Friend: So if a person says, "You're smiling too much", how do I respond?

Demario: Depends on the person. If the person is very serious and would be offended by any type of humor then you just keep a straight face, but without frowning.

Demario: I love being funny. But, some people take my humor the wrong way and it offends them. Therefore, without being rude or mean I have to be relatively quiet around some people so as to not offend them. I want to make the lives of people better, not worse. So, if my humor is affecting someone in a negative way then I will turn it off for that person and then turn it back on for the next person in line.

Friend: You should write a book. "Techniques to Deal with Negative people".

Chapter 1: Relationships

Demario: Thank you for the advice. I'm currently working on two books but dealing with negative people could be the third one.

Friend: Yes! Please help Planet Earth.

Friend: You are an inspiration in my life.

Friend: I remember that day, LOL you said, "when he gets off his rectangular device (cell phone), then we can speak!" Haha.

Friend: You handle negative energy like a genius. He was so rude and disrespectful.

Demario: It is a gift from my Creator. He lives inside of me and I let Him respond in love to people who respond to me with hatred. That's what Jesus did and that's what I do.

Demario: It wasn't the rude gentleman, it was Satan. It was a test for me. A test to see if I would love God with all of my heart and love my neighbor as myself or if I would take the easy road and respond with negativity (1 Peter 4:12).

Demario: I have a reward waiting for me in Heaven so the way people treat me is of little importance to me. I'm going somewhere and regardless of how they treat me I know that my God loves me. He loved me enough to send His only Son to die for me and that is all that matters (2 Timothy 4:8).

Friend: That's just fascinating how you rotate negativity inside your brain while making eye contact with someone.

Demario: My Jesus created me with the ability to choose, I choose positivity!

Demario: I read the end of the book, Revelation, and the secret is out... We win! We win! (Revelation 20:10; Revelation 20:15).

The God I Know

Loves you so much that He gave his only Son to die in your place (John 3:16). Jesus died to bring unity among His people, not division. Several types of relationships exist in our lives and since they involve interacting with others, we have an obligation to show the love of Christ.

Chapter 2: Progeny

Children are an inheritance from the Lord. They are a reward from him. The children born to a man when he is young are like arrows in the hand of a warrior. Blessed is the man who has filled his quiver with them. He will not be put to shame when he speaks with his enemies in the city gate. (Psalm 127:3-5 GW).

Is it just me or has the handbook for raising children changed since the seventies? Yes, you're right! The handbook changed! That coveted document that nurses and doctors continuously exclude from hospital discharge packets! My wife and I have 3 beautiful girls with very different personalities. At the beginning of our parenting journey I was determined to raise our children "exactly" how I was raised. There's humor in that confession alone, without any assistance from the various examples that could appropriately flood the page at this moment.

I was born November 20, 1976 in Tallahassee, Florida to Leroy and Sarah Rollins. I wouldn't necessarily say that my parents were strict, but I will say that I was raised in an era where a command was given and it was highly encouraged to obey, the right way, right away! Consequences were usually met with spankings of the non-abuse variety. Therefore, my younger years included corrective action designed to drive out the folly in my heart. *"Children just naturally do silly, careless things, but a good spanking will teach them how to behave"* (Proverbs 22:15 GNT). In my adolescent and teenage years I was a well behaved, thoughtful, appreciative, and reflective child. I obeyed, wisely managed allowance, excelled in school, verbally expressed appreciation and constantly thought of ways to make my parents proud. I totally skipped the whole teenage rebellion stage. (I know…aliens dropped me off and I have a lithium-ion battery pack for a power source!) So, naturally…I expected our children to obey "exactly" like I obeyed my parents. Because, that's what I "expect" and "deserve"…right? Is now the right time to tell you that "none" of my children turned out to be mirror images of the individual communicating with you at present? So, I did what any responsible dad should do…I began a quest to "make" them just like I was! Oh, what a miserable decision and what dismal consequences manifested from such a preposterous

Chapter 2: Progeny

thought! But, like yours, my parenting manual with and without updates was NOT included in any hospital discharge gift bags. I checked 3 times! NOT there!

Some of the ridiculous things I tried to do to conform my children to the image of me were:

1. Raised my voice to improve the quality and effectiveness of my commands.
2. Constantly reminded children of tasks, constantly. Did I mention I reminded them constantly?
3. Followed up on assigned tasks, constantly.
4. Gave specific time limits on assigned tasks and checked in with them along the way, constantly.
5. Expected immediate obedience to requests.
6. Expressed my disapproval of tasks performed below my expectations.
7. Expected requests to be performed exactly as I would do it.

Would now be a good time to tell you that raising children as if you are a Pharisee is not a good idea? *Parents, don't be hard on your children. Raise them properly. Teach them and instruct them about the Lord.* (Ephesians 6:4 CEV). Jesus said that Pharisees pile up heavy burdens on people's shoulders and won't lift a finger to help (Matthew 23:4). Instead of allowing God to conform our children to the image of his Son

(Romans 8:29), I was on a Pharisaic path to conform our children to the image of me!

One of the things I have learned to love about marriage and kids is that, if you're open minded and willing to receive feedback, you have an amazing opportunity to see a reflection of your progress on the journey towards holiness. Immediate family members have a front row seat into the true character you display on a daily basis. If we are unwilling to be honest with ourselves we have a unique set of individuals who could give us insight into our parenting behaviors. Necessary to obtain truthful observations would, of course, be a zone of safety where the family member can be completely honest and truthful without being interrupted, blamed, retaliated against, or expected to experience any other untoward consequences for the constructive feedback they offer. This also means that the person receiving the feedback needs to be ready and willing to receive feedback with emphasis on listening and taking notes, with readiness to create an action plan that becomes effective immediately. The action plan must then be executed in love with grace toward those he or she has hurt or offended by previous actions. Furthermore, the hearer, in humility, must be willing to repent and ask for forgiveness for previous words and actions that caused hurt, pain, or any feelings of negativity.

Before I tell you the feedback I received I do think it necessary to mention that parenting is a tough job. To

Chapter 2: Progeny

reiterate, "NO MANUAL AVAILABLE!" There are many exceptions, but in general, parents do the best that they can with the resources they have and often structure their parenting style from their own past positive and negative experiences. I didn't purposely set out to exasperate our children or disobey scripture in the process. I just wanted our kids to be like me because I thought that I was a pretty good kid. So, my intentions were good but my method and expectations were unwarranted. An important point to remember is that communication involves both transmission and reception. I intended to transmit words, actions, and expressions designed to improve the behavior of our precious girls. However, when my words, actions and expressions were received...they were processed by those precious minds in a contrary fashion. So, communication has a lot to do with how the recipient perceives the message we're trying to send. Complicated, right? Complex, but possible! So, here's the feedback I received secondary to my efforts to "fix" our children:

1. "You're nice for a few seconds and then you become firm very quickly."
2. "If things don't go your way you get upset."
3. "You're away a lot because of work and when you're here you're firm with the kids."
4. "You teach out of the Bible but they're not going to want to hear what you have to say until they know you care."

5. "If you're firm with the kids too much, when they get older they're not going to want to talk to or be around you and that's not what you need."
6. "You're always telling them to stop talking because it's past bedtime, they don't get to enjoy you."
7. "Although you teach them about love from the Bible's perspective, you do not consistently model it in a way that they can see it in action."

It was eye opening and humbling to hear how I was perceived from the ones who were able to see my attempt to parent on a daily basis. I didn't interrupt. I didn't try to defend myself. I didn't give excuses for my actions. Even if the "perception" was a great distance from my "intention" or even my own personal assessment, my purpose was to take the information and create an action plan and implement change, immediately! *Children are a gift from the Lord; they are a real blessing.* (Psalm 127:3 GNT). Therefore, it behooves parents to invest in biblical study, seminars, counseling, parenting literature, and other resources that can help us to fill in the huge gap between the way we were raised and the strategies available to help with raising this new generation. I have experience in all of the avenues previously shared but my greatest resource secondary to God's Holy Word is my dear wife Heather D. Rollins (A.K.A. Flower).

Chapter 2: Progeny

Here are some of the pearls she has shared with me on my journey to be a better dad:

1. "Don't leave the house without saying goodbye individually to all family members."
2. "Don't come home and start correcting, let 'limited' time be 'valuable' time."
3. "Be calm, don't always react to childish behavior, they are 'children', you know."
4. "Listen to your children and be there for them. Be present."
5. "Hug, kiss, and say 'I love you' as often as time and acceptance will allow."
6. "Don't act or speak out of anger. Correct yes, but always in love."
7. "Don't be afraid to show affection to your daughters, better from you than they seek it elsewhere."
8. "Don't be upset when things don't go the way you planned. Like a GPS, reroute & keep on going."

With lots of prayer and help from the indwelling Holy Spirit, I have become more proficient at projecting love and our children actually "perceiving" my words, actions, and expressions in the same way I'm "transmitting". I saved a text message from my wife that comforts my spirit because it reminds me that the effort we put forth to allow God to change us from the inside out affects those around us for the good!

"I am 100 % in love with you. You make me smile, you make me laugh. You make me want to be a better daughter of the Heavenly King! You are the fun in the family according to a little six year old who said this morning that 'days without daddie...we just don't laugh as much...' Your integrity is astounding. You've built such a wonderful character to demonstrate to our children. I'm thankful each day for your decision to come to Arkansas to begin and continue a life together. I'm thrilled to call you my husband and I'm so glad that I get to spend the rest of my life with you. It's an honor to stand by your side each day serving our Lord in all that we do. I love you and I'm thinking of you. I can't wait to see you tonight! Thank you for kissing me in the mornings before you leave...means the world to me."—Flower

Always remember that the words you say, how you say them, when you say them, and the expression you use while communicating play a vital role in your transmission being received appropriately with love and grace. **Timing. Words. Tone. Expression.**

Before closing this chapter I'd like to share a few outros with you from the annals of interactions with our children:

07-31-15:

Chapter 2: Progeny

Makayela: "Dad, did you know that if you get plastic surgery you can't go outside?"
Dad: "No Makayela, I didn't know that."
Makayela: "Yea, because they're plastic...I had a Barbie once and she was plastic. I left her outside and when I came back her foot was flat. It was bubbly but the bubbles had burst and her foot looked really funny!"

11-17-15:

Makayela: "Dad, I need another laundry basket. My clothes are overflowing. They overflew 2 days ago."

Circa 2015: I noticed my middle daughter Maddie playing with a measuring tape. I asked her to put the measuring tape down and from what I could ascertain, she was motioning to obey. I entered the bathroom only to hear the sound of measuring tape again. I exclaimed through the door, ", Maddie, I thought I told you to put the measuring tape down." And then came the reply through the door…"I did put it down, and then I picked it back up again."

The God I Know

<u>*Intends for our children to be a blessing to us*</u>. Regardless of the circumstances preceding their birth, they were always "expected" in the eyes of the Lord

from the foundation of the world. If He allowed the birth to occur then we must trust that He has purpose for the eternal soul and the temporal flesh that He chose to knit together in the womb. Let us pray for and cherish His creations as parents who assume the role of steward with integrity and patience.

Chapter 3: Depression

"It is so sad but I only know where I have been and where I am. I have no idea where I am going or for the matter of it...where I want to go. I have no hopes, I have no dreams, and I have no meaning that I am aware of. This is my loneliness and this is my depression."

AND I THOUGHT EVERYTHING WAS OKAY
10/24/99 (22 years 11 months 4 days old)
By: Demario L. Rollins

"Here I sit...bored out of my mind, mixed with a little bit of depression. It seems that all I am good for is either bringing people way up or bringing them way down. As much as I love myself, sometimes I hate myself and as much as I hate myself sometimes I accept myself, and as much as I accept myself sometimes I wonder who it is I really am and how I came to be this way. I very rarely think of suicide or moving to a distant state or country to start a new life. Oftentimes I just wonder why it is so hard for me to accept people for who they are. Why is it that I look for perfection when I myself am not even close to it?

I am so empty inside...no fear, no love, no hate, and no emotion. I hate being this way because this is not how the Creator intended it to be. Is there anything wrong with admitting that you are lonely? I find it hard to do so because I want everyone to think that I can make it along quite well without them, when in fact it is their presence that keeps me going. I want to be real with people but I don't know which one of my personalities to single out and stick to. I am so close to so many people yet so far away from the same individuals.

And where is it shall I go from here? And who is it that I shall tell of that destination? It is so sad but I only know where I have been and where I am. I have no idea where I am going or for the matter of it...where I want to go. I have no hopes, I have no dreams, and I have no meaning that I am aware of. This is my loneliness and this is my **depression.** I search for people and places that do not exist. I search for personalities without flaw, I search for a world that has yet to come and still I am quite undone in present imperfection."

From the outside everything looked great! I was surrounded by family, friends, and had a bright future. In fact, I was only 260 days away from being presented with a Doctor of Pharmacy degree at the ripe old age of twenty-three. How is it that someone who had so much going for them can pen words of dismay that seem to

Chapter 3: Depression

tell a different story concerning the inner world? Here are three responses from three different people aged **16**, **29**, and **54** who were recently permitted to read what I had written.

Age **16**: "I totally can relate to what you wrote. That's exactly how I feel sometimes!"

Age **29**: "Can you send me a copy of that!?!? I know how I feel inside but I haven't been able to put it into words. I want to tweak it just a bit and give it to my psychiatrist!"

Age **54**: "Does that have my name tagged at the end of it?"

I surmise that there are many among us who wear the facade of mostly sunny, eighty-six degrees Fahrenheit, zero chance of rain, and a mild breeze barely exceeding four miles per hour when really it is cataclysmically, cyclonically, and tumultuously terrible on the inside. Where did we learn to hide so well? Perhaps it was in the Garden of Eden after The Fall. We've been hiding ever since!

Depression in its most basic definition as expressed by Merriam-Webster is a state of feeling sad. By contrast, *Clinical* Depression as expressed by Merriam-Webster and Google is a mental health disorder characterized by persistently depressed mood or loss of interest in activities, causing significant impairment in daily life. Clinical depression manifests itself by characteristics such as sadness, inactivity, difficulty in thinking and concentration, significant increase or

The God I Know

decrease in appetite and time spent sleeping, feelings of dejection and hopelessness and sometimes suicidal tendencies. This chapter in no fashion attempts to delineate, explain, fix, treat, discredit, minimize, or eschew clinical depression. In fact, having been in the medical field since 1999 has given me a unique appreciation and respect for mental anomalies and their effect on the human psyche. To that end, we will elaborate on strategies helpful in depression not associated with that which has been selectively termed Clinical Depression. What I would like to accomplish here is an extension of a concept previously alluded to in Chapter 1 on relationships. To get started, let's take a look at an excerpt:

"Not many of our valued guests offered positive words or delightful gestures. Nevertheless, I brought my own joy to work with me and **did not permit my outward circumstances to infiltrate the fun-filled carnival going on internally**. One of the customers who witnessed my unfortunate encounters with the mean-spirited public and the overwhelming circumstances under which we were working complimented me on the way I was handling the situation. **I told her that I was able to smile, laugh, and keep a positive attitude because of Jesus.**"

The focus of Chapter 1 was loving others as we love ourselves and offering the recurring service called "auto-forgiveness". When it comes to gaining the advantage over the debilitating emotion called

Chapter 3: Depression

depression, the focus shifts to the battleground of our own minds. *The weapons we use are not human ones. Our weapons have power from God and can destroy the enemy's strong places. We destroy people's arguments, and we tear down every proud idea that raises itself against the knowledge of God. We also capture every thought and make it give up and obey Christ.* (2 Corinthians 10:4-5 ERV).

On any given day we have at least three negative forces coming against us: Satan, Society, and Self. These can often intertwine and be difficult to differentiate. The focus for the rest of this chapter will be on **Self.**

Satan: *The thief comes only in order to steal, kill, and destroy.* (John 10:10a GNT).

Be alert, be on watch! Your enemy, the Devil, roams around like a roaring lion, looking for someone to devour. (1 Peter 5:8 GNT).

Society: *Do not love the world or anything that belongs to the world. If you love the world, you do not love the Father. Everything that belongs to the world— what the sinful self desires, what people see and want, and everything in this world that people are so proud of—none of this comes from the Father; it all comes from the world.* (1 John 2:15-16 GNT).

Self: the voice of voices that provides a seemingly endless flow of narration to the inner self concerning all things relevant to the outer world. This is the voice that has been quoted as saying things such as:

"You can't do that."

"You're a failure."
"You're not good enough."
"You're overweight."
"You're not pretty enough."
"You'll never_____."

...and the list goes on into virtual infinity. As previously mentioned, when it comes to gaining the advantage over the debilitating emotion called depression, the focus shifts to the battleground of our own minds. In 2 Corinthians 10:5, the Word of God declares that *we tear down every proud idea that raises itself against the knowledge of God. We also capture every thought and make it give up and obey Christ.* (ERV).

Don't ask why, but I enjoy vacuuming. Hesitant to cross over into iRobot Roomba land and too frugal to become a Dyson owner, I settled for a Hoover WindTunnel Air Bagless Upright Vacuum cleaner which is lightweight, maneuverable, and best of all, less than $150.00! I was diligent and faithful to empty the dirt canister, clean the bristles, and rinse the ONE filter located at the top of the transparent WindTunnel dirt canister. Then, one day I pressed a button that I'd never pressed before and a magical compartment opened to display a SECOND filter that refused to display ANY sign of cleanliness. I began using the vacuum cleaner in 2013 and it wasn't until 2018 that I realized it had TWO filters! It was completely BLACK with 5 years of trapped particles that were banished from remaining affixed to our home living spaces for more than 1825 days! I've never seen a filter live up to its name and purpose as well as this one. Note to self: "You should have read the manual".

I believe God's Word is a lot like those HEPA filters on my Hoover. Dirt, debris, dust, and thousands of particles are drawn into the machine and trapped into fine mesh. As we hear the inner voice make suggestions to our mind we need to trap the dirt of lies, the debris of doubt, and the dust of our nature and the thousands of particles that bombard us each day and filter them through the Word of God. Through a healthy intake of God's Word on a daily basis, you will agglomerate such a complex labyrinth of "verse filters" that you will ***not permit the outward circumstances to infiltrate the fun-filled carnival you have going on internally.***

(Note: Fun-filled carnival is the "code name" I've given to the joy I experience as a result of Jesus' death on the cross for my sins and the free gift of eternal life I've been given)

Jesus told us plainly in John 16:33 that we will have many trials and sorrows. But He also told us to take heart, be brave, and cheer up because He has overcome the world.

So, how do we "***not permit the outward circumstances to infiltrate the fun-filled carnival we should have going on internally?***"

Well, let me present you with some Bible characters, scriptures, and perspectives that help me filter life's circumstances through the truth of God's Word.

Job

There was a man in the land of Uz, whose name was Job; and that man was blameless and upright, one who feared God, and turned away from evil. (Job 1:1 RSV).

The Lord said to Satan, "Very well, all that he has is in your power; only do not stretch out your hand against him!" So Satan went out from the presence of the Lord. (Job 1:12 NRSV).

After Job heard all these reports, he got up and tore his robe. He shaved his head. Then he fell to the ground and worshiped the Lord. He said, "I was born naked. And I'll leave here naked. The Lord has given, and the Lord has taken away. May the name of the Lord be praised." In spite of everything, Job didn't sin by blaming God for doing anything wrong. (Job 1:20-22 NIRV).

The Lord blessed the last part of Job's life even more than the first part. Job had fourteen thousand sheep, six thousand camels, a thousand teams of oxen, and a thousand female donkeys. (Job 42:12 EXB).

Job lived a life that was pleasing to God. The hardships he experienced was not because he was being punished, but rather, being bragged upon. Could it be that the trials and tribulations we face are sometimes a compliment from the One who sends or allows them? Job's story reminds me that bad things do happen to good people and sometimes it's a sign that we are on the right track.

Chapter 3: Depression

Joseph

*This is the family history of Jacob. Joseph was a young man, **17 years old**. He and his brothers cared for the flocks. His brothers were the sons of Bilhah and Zilpah, his father's wives. Joseph gave his father bad reports about his brothers.* (Genesis 37:2 ICB).

*When some Midianite traders passed by, they drew Joseph up, lifting him out of the pit, and **sold him** to the Ishmaelites for twenty pieces of silver. And they took Joseph to Egypt.* (Genesis 37:28 NRSV).

***And the Lord was with Joseph**, and he was a prosperous man; and he was in the house of his master the Egyptian.* (Genesis 39:2 KJV).

*And Joseph's master took him and put him into the **prison**, the place where the king's prisoners were confined; he remained there in prison.* (Genesis 39:20 NRSV).

***But the Lord was with Joseph**, and shewed him mercy, and gave him favour in the sight of the keeper of the prison.* (Genesis 39:21 KJV).

*"Look!" Pharaoh confirmed to Joseph, "I've put you **in charge** of the entire land of Egypt!"* (Genesis 41:41 ISV).

*And Joseph was **thirty years old** when he stood before Pharaoh king of Egypt. And Joseph went out from the presence of Pharaoh, and went throughout all the land of Egypt.* (Genesis 41:46 KJV).

*And now don't be grieved or angry with yourselves for **selling me** here, because God sent me ahead of you to preserve life.* (Genesis 45:5 CSB).

*"Therefore it was not you who sent me here, **but God**. He has made me a father to Pharaoh, lord of his entire household, and ruler over all the land of Egypt."* (Genesis 45:8 HCSB).

Though Joseph hadn't done anything to deserve all that he experienced, he kept a positive attitude because he knew that the God of the Universe was with him. God had a plan for him. He was hated by his brothers, sold into slavery, accused of rape, and thrown into prison. He had ample opportunity to be depressed. I imagine he filtered his circumstances through the spectrum of the One True God and what he knew to be true about Him. So, when you're going through a season of your life that would lead you to believe that God has abandoned you, perhaps Emmanuel (God with us) is preparing you for the purpose for which you were created.

(Note: **bold** print added for emphasis)

Romans 8:28

And we know [with great confidence] that God [who is deeply concerned about us] causes all things to work together [as a plan] for good for those who love God, to those who are called according to His plan and purpose. (The Amplified Bible).

Chapter 3: Depression

The most commonly used cake ingredients include **flour**, **sugar**, **eggs**, **butter** and **baking soda**. Individually, these ingredients in their raw form would not make for a desirable desert. However, mixed together in their appropriate portions by a skilled pastry chef and the result is a delectable delight! Likewise, the circumstances of our lives individually can acquire adjectives such as cruel, disappointing, depressing, unfair, miserable, tragic or disastrous. However, mixed together in their appropriate portions by the King of kings and Lord of lords and the result is a life well done.

1 Peter 4:12-13

Dear friends, do not be surprised at the fiery ordeal among you, when it takes place to test you, as if something strange were happening to you. But to the degree that you share in the sufferings of Christ, rejoice, so that also at the revelation of his glory you may rejoice and be glad. (LEB).

I remember being in school and the teacher would give us a syllabus at the beginning of the semester. In the syllabus, the teacher would outline everything that was expected in the weeks to come. It would describe chapters, topics, quizzes, tests, exams, final exams, and even breaks we'd have. Those who actually looked at the syllabus and followed it were prepared for what was to come. For those who ignored, lost, or misplaced their syllabus, the tests seemed <u>*unfair*</u> and <u>*unexpected*</u>

because these students were totally unprepared to take them. For those who followed the syllabus...there were no surprises! The Bible is "like" a syllabus in that it outlines what we can expect out of this life so that we aren't surprised.

Jesus

Therefore we also, since we are surrounded by so great a cloud of witnesses, let us lay aside every weight, and the sin which so easily ensnares us, and let us run with endurance the race that is set before us, looking unto Jesus, the author and finisher of our faith, who for the joy that was set before Him endured the cross, despising the shame, and has sat down at the right hand of the throne of God. For consider Him who endured such hostility from sinners against Himself, lest you become weary and discouraged in your souls. (Hebrews 12:1-3 NKJV).

Through a healthy intake of God's Word on a daily basis, I've agglomerated a complex labyrinth of "verse filters". These are just 5 examples. The possibilities are endless. Depression that attempts to take up residence in your heart can be evicted by scriptures that are already living there. It truly is difficult to be depressed and **cheer**ful at the same time.

Let's obey the words of Jesus that we've already read earlier in the chapter.

Chapter 3: Depression

> *"These things I have spoken unto you, that in Me ye might have peace. In the world ye shall have tribulation, but be of good **cheer**: I have overcome the world."* (John 16:33 KJ21).

(Note: **bold** print added for emphasis)

"There is no circumstance that you see with your eyes that can't be dissolved by the knowledge of your faith."

The God I Know

<u>Created a world and called it good</u>. Sadness did not enter the world He made until it was infiltrated by sin, the work of the Devil.

The Son of God came for this purpose: to destroy the devil's work. (1 John 3:8b NCV).

Delight yourselves in God, yes, find your joy in him at all times. Have a reputation for gentleness, and never forget the nearness of your Lord. Don't worry over anything whatever; tell God every detail of your needs in earnest and thankful prayer, and the peace of God which transcends human understanding, will keep constant guard over your hearts and minds as they rest in Christ Jesus. (Philippians 4:4-7 J.B. Phillips New Testament).

Chapter 4: Loneliness

"It is sad but perhaps true that the rejection I have received throughout the course of my life has played an *instrumental* role in the *song of dismay* my life is now *recording*."

"THERE IS LONELY"
9/23/99 (22 years 10 months 3 days old)
by: Demario L. Rollins

"The major problem I have is that I do not feel that anybody truly accepts me for who I am. Even those who try to accept me are shunned from the presence of gaining further knowledge. This is done by none other than myself. When I am single, I am comfortable with who I am, my likes, my dislikes, my fears, disappointments, triumphs, insecurities, doubts, hang-ups, and especially the secrets that are scattered throughout my mind. When I am in a relationship, I end up losing myself to the challenge of attempting to please the other person for fear of rejection of what it is that actually pleases me. This results in my unhappiness because I realize that I am unable to be myself in their presence assuming that they could not or would not accept that which comprises my total personality and character. From this problem alone stems other issues that further complicate matters. *Jealousy* becomes an issue for not feeling that I am completely loved or accepted. *Insecurity* becomes an issue for fear that the next person is better qualified for a position that has been designated as my own. Regardless of reassurance the problem persists because the real battle is within my being.

Prior to this revelation it had been my understanding that the reason I push people away was because of the relationship from my past that had broken my heart. It is now apparent to me that I push people away and keep to myself because it is only in the comfort of ME that I feel I can truly "live" and be myself. It is sad but perhaps true that the rejection I have received throughout the course of my life has played an *instrumental* role in the *song of dismay* my life is now *recording.*

Could this be why I wish not to marry? Could this be why I want to be alone for the rest of my life? Could this be how I came to be such a great entertainer?—Because there was so much to hide—Could this be why I can be so cold-hearted at times? Could this be why I run from anyone's attempt to get to know me? Could

Chapter 4: Loneliness

this be why I have yet to understand myself? Could this be why I feel like the only *close friends* I have are inanimate objects and the GREAT LORD ABOVE? Could this be why talking to myself seems to be the extent of what one would call, "expressing myself"? Could this be why I can feel like the only lonely soul in a room filled with comforting spirits? Could this be?"

[1]Lonely [**lohn**-lee] lone; solitary; without company; companionless.

I am well acquainted with loneliness. I know what it's like to be surrounded by people and still feel like the room is emptier than the words people try to use to comfort you. I want to take you on a short literary trip. It may seem irrelevant but stick with me.

Which came first...God or the Earth? Which came first...the invisible or the visible? Which will outlast the other...God or the Earth? Which will last longer...the invisible or the visible? Could it be that what we think is true, certain, tangible, and real is actually but a passing expression of God's wonderful creation? Could it be that the "invisible" is what we should consider true, faithful, trustworthy, and "real"? Invisible things were here before visible things were created and they will be here after physical things have been consumed by God's wrath. Perhaps what we can't see, and what we believe by faith should be what we believe is "true". We walk by Faith and not by sight (2 Corinthians 5:7)

The feeling of loneliness is just that. A feeling. Feelings are a wonderful and blessed part of the human experience. However, you are not a body that has a soul, you are a soul that has a body. *Therefore, if anyone is in Christ, he is a new creation; the old has passed away, and see, the new has come!* (2 Corinthians 5:17 CSB). The new man has the ability through the power of the Holy Spirit to "choose" a reality vastly different from the suggestion of the senses. In other words, when circumstances scream loneliness while the Holy Spirit whispers His promised presence, the new creation accepts the whisper in the face of what seems to be physically obvious. Furthermore, the Bible says:

But you have come to Mount Zion, to the city of the living God, the heavenly Jerusalem. You have come to thousands upon thousands of angels in joyful assembly, to the church of the firstborn, whose names are written in heaven. You have come to God, the Judge of all, to the spirits of the righteous made perfect, to Jesus the mediator of a new covenant, and to the sprinkled blood that speaks a better word than the blood of Abel. (Hebrews 12:22-24 NIV).

Close your eyes, block out the world, and breathe in this truth while exhaling the lies and deceit of the cursed Dragon. Satan and Self have a very different agenda than the Savior. **Loneliness can only be as *empty* as it vows when it is *full* of attention from you**. Escaping the snares of loneliness requires a battle.

Chapter 4: Loneliness

Although we live in the world, we don't fight our battles with human methods. Our weapons that we fight with aren't human, but instead they are powered by God for the destruction of fortresses. They destroy arguments, and every defense that is raised up to oppose the knowledge of God. They capture every thought to make it obedient to Christ. (2 Corinthians 10:3-5 CEB).

Even in the absence of physical human beings, by faith you can know, accept, and believe that you are surrounded by Jerusalem, angels, the church, God, spirits, and Jesus. And if that's not enough, you are indwelt by the Holy Spirit if you have been born again.

So the king sent horses and chariots there with a strong army. They came at night and surrounded the city. Elisha's servant got up early and went out. He saw an army with horses and chariots surrounding the city. His servant said to Elisha, "Oh, no! Master, what will we do?" "Don't be afraid," Elisha said, "because there are more of us than there are of them." Then Elisha prayed, "Lord, please open his eyes that he may see." Then the Lord opened the servant's eyes, and he saw that the mountain was full of horses and fiery chariots surrounding Elisha. (2 Kings 6:14-17 CEB).

Sometimes our eyes are so true to their purpose that they rob us of the power we have to see without them. Instead of seeing loneliness with the eyes of your body, choose to experience the perpetual presence of God with the knowledge of your soul.

The God I Know

Says He'll never leave or forsake you. He will always be under, over, and completely around you. Let this truth completely infiltrate your psyche in such a manner that it will be rendered virtually impossible to believe anything other than:

For the Lord God is one, and so are we, for we share in one faith, one baptism, and one Father. And He is the perfect Father who leads us all, works through us all, and lives in us all! (Ephesians 4:5-6 TPT).

For in Him we live, and move, and have our being. (Acts 17:28a KJV).

Where could I go to escape from you? Where could I get away from your presence? If I went up to heaven, you would be there; if I lay down in the world of the dead, you would be there. If I flew away beyond the east or lived in the farthest place in the west, you would be there to lead me, you would be there to help me. (Psalm 139:7-10 GNT).

Just as Riftia Pachyptila find their atmosphere of life and survival in the Pacific Ocean, so we, the pinnacle of 6th day creation, find our breath, life, motion, and absolute viability in the infinite grace and presence of The Most High. Because He is, we are. He gave breath to Adam and that exchange has continued from human to human and quite realistically, though it has been thousands of years, it's His breath in our lungs!

Chapter 5: Purpose

"My purpose is to encourage, inspire, and instruct others to understand, appreciate, and express the love given to us by the Father through the sacrifice of Jesus Christ by first inspiring them to have hope through laughter, joy, and forgiveness but ultimately by accepting Jesus Christ as Lord and Savior by the empowerment of the Holy Spirit."

"To Scream And Not Be Heard"

(A dismal literary work by Demario L. Rollins ... January 4, 1996)

Pain, Oh pain, why do you hurt so **bad**
Internally, yes, internal is where I'm **sad**

I scream and I scream, but to whom am I **known**
I scream and I scream, but to whom am I **shown**

The God I Know

I want out of here, I shall do away with this **life**
Oh no, I can't, I must endure this agony and **strife**

Why can't anyone hear me, I want to be **heard!!**
Why can't I just escape it all with the wings of a **bird**

I'm just a child in this world with a *purpose* **unseen**
Why won't they tell me what this life is supposed to **mean**

How does it feel to scream and not be **heard**
You don't want to know, you'd rather be the **bird**

Just give me an opportunity for happiness, and it's **mine**
Give me something to look forward to, something **divine**

I want answers to all I do not **know**
I want someone to hear me when my tears **flow**

I cry and I cry, but from whom shall my rescue **come**
I cry and I cry, but from whom shall I expect to wipe **some**

Nobody cares about me, nobody can even **hear**
Where in this world is found someone that is **sincere**

Someone that cares enough 4 me that the tears, screams, and pains **cease**
Someone that allows the love to carry on without the worry of a **lease**

Chapter 5: Purpose

I want Love...is that too much to ask from this land I **live**
I want to be heard when I scream, yet still be able to **forgive**

"Dreams I Could Never Have"

(A dismal literary work by Demario L. Rollins ... February 22, 1996)

I was born into this world just like **you**
I have two eyes, 10 fingers, and one left **shoe**

But one thing I do not is a *purpose* to guide my **way**
I am constantly reminded of this phenomenon **everyday**

I compare myself to others and am seldomly a **winner**
It seems the more time I put into anything, the more I'm a **beginner**

Why was I born into opposition that I wish with not to **compete**?
Why was I born into a world where there's so much room for **defeat**?

I don't know what to do, I've failed more than the days I've been **around**
The more I keep on living the more I continue to go **down**

The God I Know

As I look around at the success that seems to invite others to **partake**
It only makes me feel my pains worse, ending in a terrible **heartache**

Dreams are wonderful, but they are only for a select **few**
Dreams aren't meant for everyone, maybe not even for **you**

You can hope and wish, as I have tried so often to **do**
If it wasn't meant to be, then you'll be the only one loving **you**

My advice to you is none that you should give another in **need**
For I would say "Give it all up and **leave**"

If you've tried then what else to this world can you **give**?
Everybody can't be on top, so just accept your place and **live**

Maybe you're exceptional, one who success and happiness was destined **upon**
Well, I'm happy for you … apparently we are not under the same light of **sun**

My life, it's over until they tell me what's **left**
My life, it's done, I did my **best**
My life, it's one that started with many **dreams**

Chapter 5: Purpose

My life, it's one that ended without what it **seemed**
My life, I tried to love it, but it hated **me**
My life, I tried to reason with it, but could never **see**

***Love, Happiness, Success, Respect*, or even a *Reason* to live...**
Dreams I Could Never Have

Subject: **You Are Special, My Love**
Date: 12/29/02 3:46:09 PM Eastern Standard Time
From: Mom
To: Demario

My Darling Demario:

After Dominic was about four years old, we thought it would be nice to have another baby. Dominic always came home from school and said everyone had a brother or sister except him. He wanted a baby brother. Unfortunately, we weren't successful at bringing another baby into the world.

Months passed by, and I became ill at times. Lots of abdominal pain. I began experiencing infections of my ovaries and uterus. I was administered medications of all kinds to offset surgery. I told the doctor I wanted to have another child. I would get better until the next month, and the same symptoms would occur.

Finally, I didn't experience sickness for a long time. Gee, what a relief!

Oh, my. The sickness recurred after a couple of years. Back to the doctor's office. That's when the news came that my uterus would not hold another baby. It was too infected and swollen. I went to see another doctor. To no avail, I was told the same thing. Couldn't carry another baby without serious complications. I was told, though, if I became pregnant, I probably wouldn't carry full-term. I was very ill, but the doctor didn't recommend surgery (Glory to God). The pain got worse one month. I visited the doctor once more to hear both ovaries were very infected. I was told to take antibiotics for the last time, to try and get well enough to think about surgery. After taking medications, the pain subsided until the next month (just look at God). Next month, same sickness. Barely walking, I had to take another trip to Dr. McWilliams' office (in full-force pain, couldn't eat). Tests were run to determine the extent. Dr. McWilliams came back into the room, eyes stretched wide, not knowing how to tell me that I was pregnant. "PREGNANT", I said. He looked worried, and it frightened me. I asked him if he was sure. Leroy and I were thinking about taking a trip to New York, since we had given up on having children. He said, "Yes, very much pregnant". He said I would have to come in often to keep check on the uterus and the baby. They started

Chapter 5: Purpose

me off on all kinds of vitamins and medications for a healthy pregnancy.

Leroy was shocked, but very excited. We were in very good financial standings. Bills were paid off, and we really could afford to have another child. I prayed to God for you (constantly). I read to you, sang to you, and did everything that an expectant mother could do for her unborn child. Your room was all ready before you were born. You had everything. Dominic was so excited.

Everyone told me I was having a girl. Pregnancy was very good. The doctor was amazed how my uterus and ovaries repaired to carry you (just look at God).

Finally, time for delivery. Your father was due to go into the delivery room with me for your birth. They hooked me up to a monitor to make sure everything was going ok. Contractions were on time. The moment came that everyone hoped wouldn't. Contractions started going backwards instead of forward. You began losing oxygen. I wanted to have you naturally. That meant no medications to help delivery. The doctor waited as long as he could for you to deliver. No success. You just wouldn't come out. I heard the doctor say you would die if they didn't perform a C-Section to get you out. The monitor showed complications. No oxygen was getting to you. They sent Leroy out immediately, and started preparing me for surgery. They brought the oxygen mask and placed it over my face to save you. Nothing was working. I began to call on the name of JESUS. I prayed for GOD to allow me to have you naturally without surgery, and for you to be safe and healthy.

God's moment of truth came. I felt you trying to move again, trying to push your way into the world. I called the nurse to let her know, and she thought I was lying. She said, "No way." I called for the doctor. He said, "No way. Prepare her for surgery." I screamed one last time that you were coming out. The doctor checked me. His eyes stretched so wide, and everyone started running around to deliver you. I laughed and looked above to tell God "thank You". Moments later, God's miracle entered the world. Beautiful, normal, and precious as ever.

Two weeks home, your eyes were swollen and puffy. It was freezing outside. We had to take you to the doctor. Immediately, they determined it was allergies. They administered medication to your eyes, and the next day you were better. That happened several times, but the medication was very good (God needed your eyes to read His Word). A few months later, your arm (I think your right) swelled to the point you couldn't use it. You had to see a specialist for therapy, and it got better after several visits (I see why God needed your right hand–to tell others to come to Christ and

Chapter 5: Purpose

give their life—to extend the right hand of fellowship). You were a very sick child. Having allergies, when you came down with a cold, you would get pneumonia. That occurred twice.

Later in life, you began to swell, mainly your lips. That's when you had to have an allergy test performed. You were allergic to so many things. You began allergy injections. The last time you swelled, it was in your throat. I rushed you to the emergency room to get an injection. They were worried that if your throat would swell again, it would cut your oxygen off, and you might not make it through (God is sooooo good). I carried you home, and you slept most of the day. I didn't realize what I was doing at the time, but as I checked on you to make sure you were breathing, I placed my hand over your throat and prayed to God to heal you from the swelling. Glory to God, that was the last time you had a problem with that. God healed you from swelling.

You see, Demario, the odds were against you, but I believe God in His infinite wisdom and power said that's My child that I will use in a mighty way one day, and I need him to live through this. He is mine. I always saw something special in you. It was always this halo about you (I believe I told you this a long time ago). I guess that was God's way of letting me know that you belonged to Him, and He would take care of you through it all.

I love you, God's special child. I pray this new year is as special as you are.

Many Blessings,
Mother

Why did I share this with you? Because I believe every soul in pursuit of God goes through a season of wondering about and wrestling with their purpose. My mother sent me this email when I was twenty-six years old and I still cherish every word as much today as I did on that Sunday afternoon. Though her words did not specifically present my purpose in crystal clear form, it encouraged me enough to know that I had a purpose and provided motivation to stay the course until my purpose found me.

Every birth is a miracle. I encourage you to inquire from a parent, friend, or relative (with knowledge of the circumstances surrounding your birth) to share some of the obstacles or setbacks that tried to impede your arrival. Perhaps there are some childhood experiences that occurred prior to your ability to remember that placed you in harm's way. There most certainly are memories you may have of your childhood where God rescued you from illness, injury, natural disasters, or death itself. You are alive today because your life has been preserved for such a time as this.

However, you are chosen people, a royal priesthood, a holy nation, people who belong to God. You were chosen to tell about the excellent qualities of God, who called you out of darkness into his marvelous light. (1 Peter 2:9 GW).

"Who knows? Perhaps you have come to a royal position for a time such as this." (Esther 4:14b LEB).

[2]Purpose [**pur**-p*uhs*] the reason for which something exists or is done, made, used, etc.

A pencil has a purpose. A baseball bat has a purpose. A washing machine has a purpose. You, dear reader, have a purpose. In the beginning we were created in the image of God to worship Him, serve Him, reign with Him, and reflect His Glory on the Earth. There are scriptures that specifically tell us God's will as it relates to His purpose for us. Three examples are as follows:

Give thanks in every situation because this is God's will for you in Christ Jesus. (1 Thessalonians 5:18 CEB).

God's will is that your lives are dedicated to him. This means that you stay away from sexual immorality. (1 Thessalonians 4:3 CEB).

For this is the will of God, that by doing good you should put to silence the ignorance of foolish people. (1 Peter 2:15 ESV).

So, we know we are to do good, give thanks, and live a life of dedication to Him. But, that seems so general. Although we have these treasured verses, this can still leave us with the same question we started out with. What is "my" purpose? It would be wonderful if God would send us a roadmap with all pertinent directions

The God I Know

leading from the cradle to the casket. However, He has chosen to permit our daily relationship with Him to be the primary means of revealing His will. Before I share a special scripture with you about finding your purpose, consider these 7 questions:

1. What are you naturally good at doing; what talents were you born with?
2. What skills have you acquired since birth that you've mastered and enjoy doing?
3. What problems in the world are you passionate about solving?
4. How would you spend your time for Jesus if you didn't have to work?
5. What ministries in the church or service opportunities pique your interest most?
6. Do you know what your spiritual gift is or what your spiritual gifts are? (Romans 12:6-8, 1 Corinthians 12:4-11, Ephesians 4:11-13, 1 Peter 4:10-11).
7. What legacy do you want to leave on Earth once you're in Heaven with Jesus?

The answers to these questions can provide a foundation for discovering your purpose.

Now, on to the special scripture.

> *And do not be conformed to this world [any longer with its superficial values*

and customs], but be transformed and progressively changed [as you mature spiritually] by the renewing of your mind [focusing on godly values and ethical attitudes], so that you may prove [for yourselves] what the will of God is, that which is good and acceptable and perfect [in His plan and purpose for you]. (Romans 12:2 Amplified Bible).

If we want to be filled with opportunities to hear from God, to know what He wants to do through us, we must divest ourselves of the robust grasp of this world. Essentially, emptying ourselves of all that is not Him, so that we can be filled with all things that are Him. Remember in Paul's second book to Timothy when he encouraged him to "fan into flame" the gift of God, which was in him (2 Timothy 1:6)? In like manner, I want to encourage you to fan into flame the gift of God that is in you. If you're reading this book then I know you are hungry for something. Something more than mediocrity. You want to leave a legacy. You want to make a difference. You want to live a life of purpose.

"Fan the Flame"

(by: Demario L. Rollins ... November 5, 2020)

I'm an introvert with spiritual gifts. I don't push my way, I don't usurp, I don't want to draw attention to myself. Periodically I've done little things for the Kingdom here and there since moving to Arkansas, but as of recent the church leadership sent an email asking that I start a discipleship group. I immediately wanted to say "no" because I wanted to continue hiding under the radar. However, my wife was extremely encouraging and enthusiastic because she knows about the gifts I possess. I remember when I was younger I would look at other gifted children of God and wonder why they would not use their gifts for the Kingdom. I would say, "if I had that gift I would...", yet here I am sitting on my own gifts...but why? Because I'm an introvert, I don't want to push my way. I don't want to force myself into someone else's life. So, I suppose this is where the landscape changed. I wasn't forcing myself into someone else's life this time. Someone of higher authority was essentially summoning and commissioning me to do so.

I've always likened myself to Moses. Like Moses, I have a stuttering problem. Like Moses, I really wanted God to find someone else. Like Moses, I really couldn't believe that God was asking "me" to do something that I didn't feel qualified for. Like Moses, I gave excuses, lots of them. But, do you remember all the training Moses had growing up as an Egyptian? Do you realize how all of the **training, reading, studying, and preparation** was making him ready for what God was calling

Chapter 5: Purpose

him to do? So, my mom tells me that she read the Bible to me before I was even born, and then there's the miraculous way I was born as doctors told her that it would not be possible that she could give birth to a second child. Then there's how readily I accepted Jesus into my life at a very young age and took leadership roles in the church even as a child. And then there's the relationship that I developed with God and prayer life that ensued in my teenage years. In my infant faith, I made a covenant with Him that "if He" allowed me to be valedictorian, "then I" would present a speech giving Him credit for it all. I remember (when I was roughly between the ages of seventeen and nineteen) walking across the college campus and heard about a Bible study that was being led by other college students. Now, that was a dream! To be a shepherd leading someone else's understanding and development in following Jesus Christ. To choose what would be taught and teaching in your own style. To challenge others to radically and randomly do wonderful things outside of the normal walk of life. That was something I was interested in! I had a small taste of this a few years later when I conducted a Bible study on the University of South Florida's campus for a brief moment in time. I enjoyed it very much! What I have come to realize is that I am very gifted. However, because they are spiritual gifts, I am not in control of them. I can't turn them on and off. I can't make the divine happen because I want to.

"But...if there is a **need**, someone that **needs** spiritual help, something is **activated** within me that **makes me** a channel for The Divine to speak, to work, and to act and I love it!"

So, needless to say, among my gifts are communicating, teaching, writing, shepherding, dreaming, creating, and making movies every day. Each day is special and we get to create it. We can create a smile on someone else's face by saying a kind word or we can create laughter that evokes tears if the joke is just good enough. We can create our day by the choices we make and the words we say. So, as I have dreamed through the years, I've thought of so many ways to be a productive Christian and to invoke others who perhaps would someday join me in Christian productivity. I took these ideas, hid them away, and pondered them in my heart the way Mary pondered Jesus' childhood (Luke 2:19). Why? Because I'm an introvert. I really am. But I'm also an extrovert. I really am.

So, back to the present. The church leadership sent an email and they selected me to assemble and lead a discipleship group. I really wanted to say no. I really did. Nevertheless, I had just finished reading a book about discipleship groups. I'm sure that wasn't related though (that was a joke). My wife was supportive (also not related), and I also have this character trait that doesn't like to disappoint people. I like to make people happy if it's within God's laws and within my power. The church leadership thought enough to select me

Chapter 5: Purpose

and they respect me as an individual and as a Christian. I couldn't let them down.

"There was a **need**, someone that **needed** spiritual help, something was **activated** within me that **made me** a channel for The Divine to speak, to work, and to act and I love it!"

July 18, 2020: (*email*) "....identified you and certain other members throughout the congregation to be leaders in setting up Disciple Groups (D-Group). Feel free to make your invite list of 3-5 men in our class to be in your D-Group. I will be praying for you as you get your groups together!"

My *first* reaction to this email was, (for lack of a more eloquent response)..."*what*!?!?!

I didn't sign up for this. I don't know anyone. I can't lead a group of men. Who would want to follow me? I'm not even going anywhere. I don't want to interrupt the schedule of others!"

My *second* reaction was silence and *fear*. Not wanting to disappoint those who thought enough to ask my participation but fearful that they had certainly chosen the wrong guy.

My *third* reaction was *reflection*. Asking myself a series of questions.

1. Didn't you tell God you would serve if asked versus seeking your own platform?
2. Haven't you wanted to lead a discipleship group since you were 17 years old?

3. Don't you have the spiritual gifts of Teaching and Shepherding?
4. Hasn't your wife been encouraging you to share your spiritual gifts?
5. Don't you have personal quotes and inspirations to share?
6. Don't you have notes saved in preparation for such a time as this?
7. Didn't you just finish reading a book emphasizing the power of small groups?

I tried to settle in my mind that I would ignore the opportunity to obey the internal nudges and obvious voice of the Living God.

But if I say, "I won't think about him, I won't speak in his name any more," then it seems as though a fire is burning in my heart, imprisoned in my bones; I wear myself out trying to hold it in, but I just can't do it. (Jeremiah 20:9 CJB).

So, I decided that "yes" was practically the only answer I could give. And after I said yes. This is really important. "*After"* I said yes. A flood, correction, a tsunami consisting of all the **training, reading, studying, and preparation** started to roll into a new wave of Christian work for the Kingdom.

July 19, 2020: (*text message*) "Lots of people are going to be blessed by you."

After reading this text message from a respected leader in the church and committing the effort of creativity to the infinite wisdom of King Jesus, I watched everything unfold through me like a flood of Living Water (John 4:10) that I could not control (see chapter 10 for details).

So, here I am, living my dream. God's dream. The dream I had walking across the college campus wishing that I had a role in God's Kingdom to be a shepherd leading someone else's understanding and development in following Jesus Christ. Not just hearing the Word and understanding it, but also putting it into practice in a real way that goes outside of the building. I had a simmer, an ignition, a pilot light inside of me and I just needed something or someone to **Fan The Flame** into a fire.

It is my belief that all Christians that have truly been born again have that little flame burning inside of them. It may take the right moment, the right person, the right time, the right situation or the right attitude to be able to **Fan The Flame** into a fire. We all have to know ourselves and find out what will push us outside of our comfort zone to get where we need to be. Not to run from our destiny, but to embrace it. One of the best ways to find our purpose is to "get involved". Sometimes we don't know how God has gifted us until we place ourselves in His service.

My prayer for you is that this book will help align you with the right moment, person, time, situation, or attitude that will fan your flame into a fire. Your purpose is waiting.

Without a clear purpose:

"To Scream And Not Be Heard"
(A dismal literary work...January 4, 1996)

"Dreams I Could Never Have"
(A dismal literary work...February 22, 1996)

With a clear purpose:

"My purpose is to encourage, inspire, and instruct others to understand, appreciate, and express the love given to us by the Father through the sacrifice of Jesus Christ by first inspiring them to have hope through laughter, joy, and forgiveness but ultimately by accepting Jesus Christ as Lord and Savior by the empowerment of the Holy Spirit."...circa 2002

The God I Know

<u>*Feels the same way about you as He did about Jeremiah*</u>. *For God does not show favoritism.* (Romans 2:11 CJB). How did He feel about Jeremiah?

"Before I made you in your mother's womb, I chose you. Before you were born, I set you apart for a special work." (Jeremiah 1:5a,b NCV).

Chapter 5: Purpose

I know the plans I have in mind for you, declares the Lord; they are plans for peace, not disaster, to give you a future filled with hope. (Jeremiah 29:11 CEB).

Chapter 6: Salvation

> "I won't be beneficial to you in spiritual matters unless you decide that you are separated from God due to sin and that the only way back to Him is through Jesus Christ."

Have you ever tried to share your faith with another individual? This, unequivocally, is a unique and potentially terrifying experience. As we venture closer to the day of Christ's return coupled with the fact that we're living in the last days (Hebrews 1:2), I have seen a shift in the hearts of those around me. *The time will come when people won't put up with true teaching. Instead, they will try to satisfy their own desires. They will gather a large number of teachers around them. The teachers will say what the people want to hear. The people will turn their ears away from the truth. They will turn to stories that aren't true.* (2 Timothy 4:3-4 NIRV).

The God I Know

While discussing the issue of salvation with a good friend who is not yet of The Way (Acts 24:14), I found myself expressing my plight in terms that I will now share with you:

"A person can't be 'saved' if they don't feel or know that they are 'lost.' Most of the world doesn't have a concept of being lost so the gospel of Jesus doesn't mean much to them. I won't be beneficial to you in spiritual matters unless you decide that you are separated from God due to sin and that the only way back to Him is through Jesus Christ. I cringe at the thought of even explaining this because this message is quite offensive to those who are not ready to receive it. Hopefully after this text you will permit the exchange of friendly words to continue throughout the years."

The good news is, the friendly texts have continued. The other news is, the friend is not yet my Sister in Christ and that pains my heart. *Brethren, my heart's desire and prayer to God for Israel is, that they might be saved.* (Romans 10:1 KJV). Dear reader, my heart's desire and prayer to God for the whole world is that they may be saved. *The Lord is not slack concerning his promise, as some count slackness; but is longsuffering to you-ward, not wishing that any should perish, but that all should come to repentance.* (2 Peter 3:9 ASV).

Six hundred and eighty eight days later I asked another young lady if she was a BODY that had a soul or if she was a SOUL that had a body. Surprisingly, she believed that she was a soul. So, I asked, "If you believe

Chapter 6: Salvation

that you are a soul, why do you reject spiritual things and cater to the needs and wants of your body?" To my dismay, the conversation ended there. Again I ask, have you ever tried to share your faith with another individual? Again I say, this, unequivocally, is a unique and potentially terrifying experience.

When we think of evangelism, it's easy to imagine that it's an elaborate and complicated act of persuasion strictly reserved for the life long Bible expert who knows the scriptures like the back of his hand. However, evangelism is every believer's job and not just a feat for the brave at heart. As a way of life, we should share the good news, the gospel, with intent to lift the name of Jesus Christ presenting Him as the Way, the Truth, the Life, and Only way to the Father (John 14:5).

Through the blood of Jesus shed on the cross for our sins, we have been redeemed and are now part of Christ's family. We want the whole world to be a part of His family too! So, as we live our lives we should make it a priority to tell other people "our story" (the journey from lost to found) because we want them to have "their own story." We want everyone to be a part of His-Story. At the heart of salvation is the gospel. There's just no way around it. Ultimately, that is our purpose. The gospel message of Jesus Christ that we have been commissioned to proclaim is the preeminent priority for the body of Christ. Besides sharing the gospel, there are a plethora of "good deeds" we can do to impact the world around us. However, God *has not* called us

The God I Know

to make Earth the best possible place from which the unsaved can die and go to Hell. God *has* called us to transform the hearts and minds of a sinful world with the power of the gospel.

Imagine for a moment that you live next door to someone you have not formally met. You may gesture at your neighbor or wave while at the mailbox, but nothing more. One day as you are arriving home late in the evening you realize that your neighbor's house has caught fire and they are inside...what would you do? (Answer: you would personally run to save them or call someone else who could. Either way, you put forth *urgent effort* to get help because in a matter of moments, all will be lost). Envision for an additional moment that you were cured from an awful disease that would have claimed your life. Each day you meet people who have the same awful disease that you used to have...what would you do? (Answer: you would personally offer them the cure that you received or you would direct them to someone else who could. Either way you put forth *urgent effort* to get help because in a matter of moments, all will be lost).

Dear brothers and sisters, the world around us is in a constant state of urgency. Their lives have caught fire with sin and their very souls are diseased with the same terminal illness (sin) we used to have before we were healed (Isaiah 53:5). It is the responsibility of the heart that has been saved by the blood of Jesus to

Chapter 6: Salvation

personally put forth an <u>*urgent effort*</u> to help them. We do this by sharing the gospel of Jesus Christ.

For I am not ashamed of the Gospel. I see it as the very power of God working for the salvation of everyone who believes it, both Jew and Greek. I see in it God's plan for imparting righteousness to men, a process begun and continued by their faith. For, as the scripture says: 'The just shall live by faith'. (Romans 1:16 J.B. Phillips New Testament).

Don't forget that you Gentiles used to be outsiders. You were called "uncircumcised heathens" by the Jews, who were proud of their circumcision, even though it affected only their bodies and not their hearts. In those days you were living apart from Christ. You were excluded from citizenship among the people of Israel, and you did not know the covenant promises God had made to them. You lived in this world without God and without hope. But now you have been united with Christ Jesus. Once you were far away from God, but now you have been brought near to him through the blood of Christ. (Ephesians 2:11-13 NLT).

We once lived in this world without God and without hope. But now that we have been united with Christ Jesus, we must accept the great commission (Matthew 28:19-20) God gave us without making excuses.

Make the most of your time because the days are evil. (Ephesians 5:16 TLV).

Here are some questions to stimulate some thoughts about your story:

1. Who introduced you to Jesus?
2. How did you come to know about Jesus?
3. How does Christianity enrich your family life?
4. Who were you before Jesus Christ saved you?
5. How is your speech different after spending time with Jesus?
6. What journey did you embark upon to discover His Amazing Grace?
7. How does your relationship with Jesus influence your daily decisions?

Before you can introduce someone to Jesus so that they will eventually have a story of their own, it is essential that you know your own story. When you see a really great movie, what's one of the first things you want to do when you exit the theater? (Answer: share the experience with someone you care about so that they can have the potential for the same joy you've had). When your life has been forever changed by the loving-kindness of our precious Savior, we should have a desire to tell someone we care about (the world).

We don't have to know the whole bible from cover to cover before we share the good news with others. For example, doctors don't know everything. If you ask them a question or present a challenge for which they have insufficient experience, they will consult literature, colleagues, or refer you to someone who can help you better. However, doctors don't avoid practicing medicine for fear that they may be asked a question

Chapter 6: Salvation

they don't know the answer to. Likewise, when sharing our story we should not let our insufficient knowledge of the Bible limit the opportunities we are given each day to share the gospel or visit with others.

Jesus spent many days and hours telling stories. You may refer to them as parables. His parables touched people in a way that shifted their minds heavenward in the direction Jesus wanted them to go. This was not manipulation. Manipulation comes from a heart with evil intentions, not a heart of love. A loving heart gently persuades the hearer because the message being presented has eternal consequences.

Imagine that I was given a seed and asked to plant it. Would it make much sense to meticulously inspect it instead? Do I truly need to understand "*how*" the seed works before I plant it? Don't get me wrong, it is a noble endeavor to take up a specialized study in areas that pique the interest or fulfil natural talents we've been given. Just ask any botanist or phytologist and they will acquiescently confirm the sheer fascination and seemingly endless discoveries awaiting the curious minds who choose the path of the perennials! Indeed, I do not need to understand "*how*" the seed works. Rather, simply planting the seed is sufficient enough to initiate a process that God assumes responsibility for bringing to fruition.

I planted, Apollos watered, but God gave the increase. So neither the one who plants nor the one who waters is anything, but only God who makes things grow. Now he who plants and he who waters work as one, but each will receive his own reward according to his own labor. (1 Corinthians 3:6-8 TLV).

But some of the seeds fell onto good, rich soil that kept producing a good harvest. Some yielded thirty, some sixty—and some even one hundred times as much as was planted! (Mark 4:8 TPT).

The seed represents the Word of God. "We" can't save anybody. God doesn't ask us to do that. He does command us to be like the farmer in Chapter 4 of Mark.

The farmer is like a person who plants God's teaching in people. (Mark 4:14 ICB).

Maybe you've tried to share your faith in the past and have been rejected, ridiculed, persecuted, or threatened. You may have decided to just "live" a good life and hope that others will see your good works and decide to follow Jesus someday. Perhaps you're waiting on someone to ask you (1 Peter 3:15) about your faith.

But you will receive power and ability when the Holy Spirit comes upon you; and you will be My witnesses [to tell people about Me] both in Jerusalem and in all Judea, and Samaria, and even to the ends of the earth." (Acts 1:8 The Amplified Bible).

God has called us to be witnesses. Have you ever seen a silent witness in a courtroom? I haven't either. The witness is a person who gives a testimony (declaration; profession) based upon what they have seen, heard, or have knowledge of through personal experience. To reiterate, at the heart of salvation is the

Chapter 6: Salvation

gospel. There's just no way around it. Ultimately, that is our purpose. The gospel message of Jesus Christ that we have been commissioned to proclaim is the preeminent priority for the body of Christ. Besides sharing the gospel, there are a plethora of "good deeds" we can do to impact the world around us. However, God <u>has not</u> called us to make Earth the best possible place from which the unsaved can die and go to Hell. God <u>has</u> called us to transform the hearts and minds of a sinful world with the power of the gospel.

You may ask, what if they don't listen to me?

When they heard Paul speak about the resurrection of the dead, some laughed in contempt, but others said, "We want to hear more about this later." That ended Paul's discussion with them, but some joined him and became believers. Among them were Dionysius, a member of the council, a woman named Damaris, and others with them. (Acts 17:32-34 NLT).

God has commissioned us to share the good news (evangelize) as a way of life. It can be challenging because some people will laugh at us in contempt and others will dismiss us until a later time. BUT...*some will join us*!

So, since we know the fear of the Lord, we are trying to persuade people. Now, we are well known by God, and I hope that we are also well known in your consciences. (2 Corinthians 5:11 EHV).

To reference two examples mentioned earlier. When we tell our story we are letting a lost world know that we had a terminal illness and our beloved Jesus cured us. When we invite others to church it's like we are calling on someone else to come alongside us and help put the neighbor's fire out before the house burns down. We are putting forth _urgent effort_ to help them.

Did you know that God is withholding the coming of Jesus because it is not His desire that anyone should perish? If that's the case, then certainly God hasn't saved "us" and left "us" here on earth to satisfy "our" own plans and desires. When we become family members with God, through the process of sanctification, we should come to love the things He loves and hate the things He hates. If His agenda includes the lost. If Jesus came to seek and save the Lost. If we were once Lost. It is only fitting that the remainder of our lives be devoted to helping Abba Father (Romans 8:15; Galatians 4:6) call the remaining kids home so that we can all be at the marriage feast celebration in Heaven (Revelation 19:9) with Jesus as he weds "The Church". Join the Father, join Jesus, and join the Holy Spirit in the "Ministry of Reconciliation" (2 Corinthians 5:11-21) by learning your story and sharing your story with others and bringing them to the House of the Lord where repentance, baptism, and salvation will forever alter the course of their eternity! When you get to Heaven, make sure it is YOUR FAULT that someone else is there too!

Chapter 6: Salvation

The God I Know

<u>*Had a plan to save us before we ever became lost*</u> (Ephesians 1:4). From the book of Genesis forward, He lovingly and strategically revealed His plan that had been previously hidden (Colossians 1:26). He passionately pursues us and desires that we pursue Him in return.

> *This grace was given to me—the least of all the saints—to proclaim to the Gentiles the incalculable riches of Christ, and to shed light for all about the administration of the mystery hidden for ages in God who created all things.* (Ephesians 3:8-9 CSB).

> *Don't overlook the obvious here, friends. With God, one day is as good as a thousand years, a thousand years as a day. God isn't late with his promise as some measure lateness. He is restraining himself on account of you, holding back the End because he doesn't want anyone lost. He's giving everyone space and time to change. But when the Day of God's Judgment does come, it will be unannounced, like a thief. The sky will*

collapse with a thunderous bang, everything disintegrating in a huge conflagration, earth and all its works exposed to the scrutiny of Judgment. (2 Peter 3:9-10 MSG).

Chapter 7: Service

> "Learn to give more and more of your daily cares to the One who cares daily for you."

It was April 24, 2016 in the parking lot of the White County Jail in Searcy, Arkansas. I was supposed to meet the chaplain to see about serving with the jail ministry. I couldn't quite determine where to enter the building, and I didn't see anyone meeting outside. I was off the hook. *"Oh well, I tried"*, I thought to myself. *"I arrived 10 minutes early and didn't see anyone so that means I get to go home, right"*? Not so. I texted the chaplain as a last-ditch effort to prove myself worthy of having attempted to serve in a very frightening branch of ministry. The chaplain responded and welcomed me to join the team. I exited the car and reluctantly took one step after the other toward the double doors that would escort me to the indoor gathering that I had expected to be outside. I stood with men and women from various churches throughout the community who were there for one purpose—to share the plan of salvation through Jesus Christ with any inmate who was willing to listen. I was placed with two gentlemen who had years of experience doing the very thing that had come to frighten me more than serpents. I couldn't believe I was actually about to do this!

Across my mind flashed Matthew 25:34-36, the very passage of scripture responsible for my presence. *Then the King will say to those on His right, "Come, you who are blessed by my Father, inherit the Kingdom prepared for you from the creation of the world. For I was hungry, and you fed me. I was thirsty, and you gave me a drink. I was a stranger, and you invited me into your home. I was naked, and you gave me clothing. I was sick, and you cared for me. I was in prison, and you visited me."* (NLT).

One of the jail ministry veterans, Richard Denney, looked at me with divine confidence and said, "Remember, they are locked in that room with you; you aren't locked in there with them." I held on to these words tighter than a novice rock climber to his life rope. We entered the pod, as they are called, and before me were over forty men whose appearance differed greatly from that of my own. I was beyond terrified! This experience caused me to trust the God of Abraham, Isaac, and Jacob in a way that I had never done before. The first thirty-three seconds post-entrance, my mind imagined being harmed in some way by the occupants of the pod. As I gave more and more of my cares to the One who cares for me, I literally felt all of my fears and apprehensions dissipate into His loving presence. Although I was physically bound behind a steel door in a secure building, I experienced a freedom and belonging like never before.

Fast Forward Six Hundred and Sixty Five days...

Sunday February 18, 2018, seemed like just another routine opportunity to serve at the jail. I asked Richard Denney if he'd like to share a lesson or listen to one. He opted to listen, and I had prepared a brief discussion concerning temptation, the faithfulness of God, and the presence and power of the indwelling Holy Spirit. As my lesson drew to a close I encouraged the gentlemen to look for the "exit" sign in their temptations (I Corinthians 10:13) and rely on the Holy Spirit to overcome their struggles. Suddenly, one inmate who had been a little cynical during the singing portion of our worship spoke up and said that he'd just continue doing dope because he was going to Hell anyway. I gently responded by suggesting that he didn't "have to go" to Hell and so the battle began. This gentleman had quite a bit of anger and resentment toward God that had been bottled up for some time because shortly thereafter he confirmed his disgust for God by inviting expletives to join his series of interrogatives. He had lots of questions about why God would allow bad things to happen to him when he didn't do anything wrong. This guy was angry, I mean, furious. He took his identification badge and thrust it toward the ground in a rage. You could see the veins in his neck bulging as he internalized words and feelings that he tried desperately not to share. He probably knew that the words and phrases he had been choosing were not the natural selection for pleasant communication with people from the church. Nevertheless, under the guidance of the Holy Spirit, we permitted him to express his anger toward God in not so pleasant terms and encouraged him to vent. Richard engaged him with stories from his own life of trouble, turmoil, loss and unanswered questions. During Richard's Spirit-led monologue you could see tears welling up in the eyes of the once enraged, hell-bound man. Next, another inmate who could see his past self in this individual gave his own personal confession about D.O.P.E. He told him, "Never to forget that D.O.P.E. stands for Devil On Planet Earth". Additionally, he shared his personal testimony about being thrown from a car and run over and explained all of the surgeries and orthopedic implants within his body that have been inserted to hold him together. Other men in our circle spoke words of encouragement and of camaraderie. Last of all, I shared the story of Job with him and persuaded him that the possibility remains that his life events could have been because God was bragging on him (Job 1:8). I concluded my lesson by telling him that "sometimes God allows us to experience tragic circumstances in our lives just so we can prevent a future suicide or homicide in another

Chapter 7: Service

life that is unprepared to handle it the way we did with God's help". With tears in the eyes of more than one of the inmates, it wasn't a stretch to say the Holy Spirit was present with us.

Before our very eyes we witnessed a heart of stone soften into a heart of flesh (Ezekiel 36:26). The man who minutes before cursed God and destined himself to Hell was now embracing us with tears and thanking us for presenting God's Word to him. It was obvious to all who God privileged to see, we were in a battle for this man's soul! It was spiritual warfare (Ephesians 6:12)! What began with blasphemy, ended in praise. The devil was defeated. The Word of God drove Satan out of that room! Why do we minister to the incarcerated? Why do we serve in various ministries within the church? For the matter of it...why do we witness at all? Because souls are at stake! There are two destinations. Heaven and Hell. We can't miss both of them. We have to fight for the souls of our future brothers and sisters. We must tell God's story! We must tell our own story! We must go to them. We must drive the Devil out of their affairs with the Word of God. Will everyone listen? No. Will everyone who listens be in agreement with what is said? No. Nevertheless, God has gifted us to be able to serve in the Body of Christ as a way of life. It can be challenging because some people will laugh at us in contempt and others will dismiss us until a later time. BUT...some will join us! *"Well, in the same way heaven will be happier over one lost sinner who returns to God than over ninety-nine others who haven't strayed away!"* (Luke 15:7 TLB).

This is just one example of many that could be told. Jail ministry is just one of various opportunities to serve. Perhaps you would enjoy visiting widows, or doing yard work for the elderly. Maybe you'd be useful in administration or finance for a local church. How about working with college students or preparing meals for the homeless? There are needs all around us. The comfort zone is a *"safe"* place but it doesn't provide the necessary environment to grow spiritually. Dare to break free from your comfort zone. Endeavor to get involved in serving. Help meet the physical and spiritual needs of your community!

Quote from Chapter Five: "One of the best ways to find our purpose is to 'get involved'. Sometimes we don't know how God has gifted us until we place ourselves in His **service**. My prayer for you is that this book will help align you with the right moment, person, time, situation, or attitude that will fan your flame into a fire. Your purpose is waiting."

Then Jesus made a circuit of all the towns and villages. He taught in their meeting places, reported kingdom news, and healed their diseased bodies, healed their bruised and hurt lives. When he looked out over the crowds, his heart broke. So confused and aimless they were, like sheep with no shepherd. "What a huge harvest!" he said to his disciples. "How few workers! On your knees and pray for harvest hands!" (Matthew 9:35-38 The Message).

The God I Know

<u>Wants us to serve within the Body of Christ</u> inasmuch as He has gifted and enabled us to do so. We are of one body and every part is important in the work of the Lord.

So we are to use our different gifts in accordance with the grace that God has given us. If our gift is to speak God's message, we should do it according to the faith that we have; if it is to serve, we should serve; if it is to teach, we should teach; if it is to encourage others, we should do so. Whoever shares with others should do it generously; whoever has authority should work hard; whoever shows kindness to others should do it cheerfully. (Romans 12:6-8 GNT).

Chapter 8: Worship

"At the heart of worship is the heart of the worshipper. A heart surrendered is a heart that is thankful. A heart that is thankful is a heart that seeks to adore the One responsible for its existence."

I now invite you to a bible study I attended where the subject is the third person in the Holy Trinity. Listen to some of the comments shared by followers of Jesus Christ:

"We don't know what to do with It (Spirit) because we understand the Father from the Old Testament and Jesus from the New Testament but we don't have a book that tells us what it looks like to express it (Spirit)."

"I can't remember the last time I felt something emotionally in church."

"Sometimes I want to lift my hands in church but I don't want to be judged."

"I'm only 23 years old so take what I have to say with a grain of salt but I feel like if my generation were to express praise to God in worship that we would be labeled as hypocritical because we don't have a specific scripture to back up what we'd be doing."

"There are one or two songs that we sing and I get choked up but I don't want to start crying all over the place or someone will wonder what's wrong with me. If I lift my hands in church I would have to worry about someone coming over to escort me out (said jokingly)."

Oh how I wanted to raise my hand, stand up, come to the front of the room and share what was on my heart! Instead of re-enacting Luke 4:29 I decided to share my heart with you instead. By the way, this is what Luke 4:29 says, *They got up, forced him out of the town, and brought him to the brow of the hill on which their town was built, so that they could throw him down the cliff.* (New English Translation).

Love the Lord your God with all your heart, with all your soul, with all your mind, and with all your strength. (Mark 12:30 HCSB).

God is a Spirit: and they that worship him must worship him in spirit and in truth. (John 4:24 KJV).

Let's go back to the five comments earlier from bible study. Does anything strike you about them? None of them entirely focus on the love relationship we have with God the Father through Jesus Christ our Lord sealed until the day of redemption by the Holy Spirit. Is worship not "shipping worth" to the object of

Chapter 8: Worship

our worship? Is worship not expressing to Abba Father the credit, fame, and allegiance that He so rightfully deserves? Is worship not a lifestyle that seeks to magnify the God-Head three in One?

Ahh, worship! The experience and privilege to come into the presence of the Most High and unashamedly expose our hearts to the only One who can heal, mend, and fill them. Worship! We are the bride of Christ, are we not? He is our husband. There is a unique and exclusive relationship involving a love like we've never known or could know apart from Christ. I'm married to a beautiful Arkansan princess who I endearingly call "Flower". Her name is Heather and what I call her expresses the meaning within her birth name. Let's say I'm attracted to Flower and I wish to show her my love. Would I do that by sitting completely still in hopes that she'd know clairvoyantly that I desire to see her exclusively? Let's say I'm married to Flower (so glad this is true) and I never embrace her, speak to her, spend time with her, or do anything more than come in her presence. Do you think Flower would appreciate the manner in which I am choosing to show her my love? Probably not because in truth, I'm not showing love at all! At the heart of worship is the heart of the worshipper. A heart surrendered is a heart that is thankful. A heart that is thankful is a heart that seeks to adore the One responsible for its existence. Behind all the distractions the enemy shoves to the forefront is the same question that always remains, what is the condition of your heart? Do we love Jesus? Do we love God? Do we love the Holy Spirit? When we love someone, I mean, really love someone, all that matters to you is what that person thinks about you. Honestly, you could care less about onlookers because your sole intent is to capture the attention, affection and affirmation of the one you're committed to love. Should we lift our hands? Should we cry? Should we dance? Should we run? We should worship the One who is able to keep us from falling. We should worship the One who is able to present us faultless before the presence of His glory with exceeding joy. We should worship the only wise God our Savior because it is to Him that glory, majesty, dominion and power belongs, both now and forever. Amen. (Jude 24).

Worship is very simple. How do you wish to express your love to the King for who He is? Are you head over heels and deeply in love with the One who redeemed you from the clutches of the adversary? Does your heart not melt with tender affection at the sound of His name? Does not every fiber of your being leap for joy at the thought of spending eternity in His presence? Alas! Show Him! Selah!

The God I Know

<u>Wants us to know that THE TIME is coming and indeed it is here NOW</u>

Chapter 8: Worship

Indeed, the time is coming, and it is now here, when the true worshipers will worship the Father in spirit and truth. The Father is looking for people like that to worship him. God is a spirit. Those who worship him must worship in spirit and truth." (John 4:23-24 NOG).

Chapter 9: Marriage

"To make marriage work you MUST take the exit door off its hinges and erect a brick wall 54 feet deep in its place that can NEVER be penetrated. Marriage requires audacious commitment and the relentless courage to be *willingly*, *sacrificially*, and safely *sequestered* in this once in a lifetime opportunity."

Marriage is one of the most wonderful and yet challenging journeys one will ever experience in this lifetime. There are many books that could be written and indeed have been written on the subject. This chapter and the headings that shall ensue may seem incoherent, incongruent, and perhaps even disjointed. This is intentional. Somewhere in the ambiguity, I pray that you will discover lucid rays of hope, pearls of wisdom, and novel ideas that will help you on your quest to improve your marriage or make better choices prior to entering this precious covenant.

I am not an expert on the subject but rather the recipient of *miles* and *kilometers* of mistakes that have helped me to arrive at a *destination* fit to express the *trip* in words.

Though the *radius* of my thoughts extend to various points within the *circumference* of the complete *circle* of marriage, I choose but one thesis. Ok, actually there are several themes throughout this chapter but one of the key points I wish to drive home is to eliminate the word "*divorce*" from existence as a noun or verb in the lives of those who choose the sacred covenant of marriage established by God. Statistics and the resident evil present in the atmosphere of our existence argue most convincingly that there will absolutely be exceptions to this bold declarative. Nevertheless, "*If possible, so far as it depends on you, be at peace with all people.*" (Romans 12:18 NASB). Yes, that includes your spouse.

*The Lord, the God of Israel, says, "**I hate divorce**, and I hate the cruel things that men do. So protect your spiritual unity. Don't cheat on your wife."* (Malachi 2:16 ERV).

Some Pharisees came and tried to trap him with this question: "Should a man be allowed to divorce his wife for just any reason?" "Haven't you read the Scriptures?" Jesus replied. "They record that from the beginning 'God made them male and female.' "And he said, "'This explains why a man leaves his father

Chapter 9: Marriage

*and mother and is joined to his wife, and **the two are united into one**.' Since **they are no longer two but one**, let no one split apart what God has joined together."* (Matthew 19:3-4 NLT).

*Jesus replied, "You are so heartless! That's why Moses allowed you to divorce your wife. But from the beginning **God did not intend it to be that way**.* (Matthew 19:8 CEV).

(Note: **bold** print added for emphasis)

After about 14,656 days of dwelling on the third sphere from the sun, I acquired an interest in the hobby of radio controlled helicopter flight. It began with curiosity concerning a $19.99 display model in a local CVS store to which my wife declined an offer to test fly in our home. Two months later I found myself unsuccessfully attempting to pilot an 18.7 inch 800mAh 3S 11.1 volt lithium polymer powered versatile flybarless aerobatic collective pitch rotor system helicopter for the intermediate pilot. What!?!?! There's a phrase that is exchanged in radio controlled helicopter forums that basically goes..."Fly. Crash. Repair. Repeat." During one of my "pretending to be an intermediate pilot episodes", I willingly confess that I was not able to deplete the battery's available power because the helicopter was no longer capable of leaving the ground without my total assistance. I looked extensively at this sophisticated mechanical device in hopes that I could repair what was wrong. I gave it the best effort any 64 day experienced helicopter mechanic could and I assure you that my contribution to the mangled mess of my human error was of no benefit to reuniting the helicopter to its native environment. I swallowed my pride and made a very profound decision that day. I decided to ship it back to the manufacturer who knew exactly how to get the helicopter back in the air. Professionals are really good at what they do! Our marriages would have the savoir-faire necessary for survival if we would but release them back into the omniscient hands of the Most High who created them. God is really good at what He does!

God created marriage. It belongs to Him as yet another wonderful gift to the human beings made in His likeness and image. The Apostle Paul is unequivocally one of the most influential Christians to serve in the Lord's army. *But whatever I am now, it is all because God poured out His special favor on me—and not without results. For I have worked harder than any of the other apostles; yet it was not I but God who was working through me by His grace* (I Corinthians 15:10 NLT). And yet with all of his spiritual gifts, knowledge, and revelations from Jesus Christ, Paul said in Ephesians 5:32 that *"marriage is a great mystery"* as he speaks of it in light of its inextricable union with Christ and the Church.

Chapter 9: Marriage

Illustration

There was an **army** who was severely outnumbered and preparing for war on an island. Knowing his fleet would retreat at the sight of the disadvantageous circumstances, the **General** set fire to all vessels used to transport the army to their current destination. Frankly, there was absolutely no escape. Before the soldiers was an enemy battalion numbering at least triple their armada. Behind them they beheld their ships billowing in flames. They found themselves *sequestered* between sabotaged ships and a spiteful squadron of able troops. Suddenly, emancipating from the vocals of the General came the command to attack. Without options and against all odds, they forged forward and fought with tenacity and reckless abandon. The few soldiers with no plan of escape, who essentially were fighting for survival, won the battle that day. Figuratively, their exit door was taken off its hinges and no way of escape was possible. Therefore, they faced the challenge of the day instead of retreating. They fought with unrivaled intensity because the situation at hand mandated such execution. The General was wise enough to metaphorically erect a brick wall 54 feet deep that could never be penetrated. His decision to remove all avenues of escape paved an unforeseen boulevard of success for the army to achieve what they thought impossible.

Explanation

There was a **married couple** who was severely outnumbered and preparing for war (1 Peter 5:8) in a world occupied by antithetical forces (Ephesians 6:12). Knowing His married couple would retreat towards divorce at the sight of disadvantageous circumstances, **God** clearly expressed His disapproval for them to ever separate from one another (Malachi 2:16) and gave them His laws in a book (2 Timothy 3:16). By doing so, He spiritually set fire to all vessels and avenues that could facilitate separation from themselves or their current situation. Frankly, there was absolutely no escape. Before the married couple was an enemy battalion numbering at least triple their relationship. Behind them they beheld all avenues leading to divorce billowing in flames. They found themselves *sequestered* between an inseparable relationship (Mark 10:8) and a spiteful squadron of able troops (Revelation 12:9). Suddenly, emancipating from the vocals of God came the command to attack. Without options and against all odds, they forged forward and fought with tenacity and reckless abandon. The married couple with no plan of escape, who essentially were fighting for survival, won the battle that day. Figuratively, their exit door was taken off its hinges and no way of escape was possible. Therefore, they faced the challenge of the day instead of retreating. They fought with unrivaled intensity because the situation at hand mandated such

Chapter 9: Marriage

execution. God in His infinite wisdom gave His Son to be crucified and His Holy Spirit to live in us to erect a brick wall 54 feet deep that can never be penetrated. God's decision to remove all avenues of escape paved an unforeseen boulevard of success for the couple to achieve what they thought impossible.

Choices

I visited https://www.chick-fil-a.com to do a little experiment (menu results subject to change). I clicked on the "menu" tab and proceeded to check out the breakfast choices. There were 16 Breakfast choices...yummy!

11 Entrees	Totally	Delectable
3 Salads	Absolutely	Enjoyable
10 Sides	Entirely	Excellent
3 Kid's meals	Fully	Fantastic
7 Treats	Positively	Flavorful
14 Drinks	Thoroughly	Refreshing

Having 64 choices of sustenance from Chick-fil-a is a remarkable reality (yes, there was some overlap, but delicious choices nonetheless). However, when it comes to marriage, having choices is not such a great situation to be in.

For example, take pizza for instance...

"I surmise that over 50% of readers have tried a minimum of 5 different types of pizza. Toppings, crust, sauce, and companies contribute to the varieties our taste buds have experienced. Because of this vast array, we have the "fortune" of being able to rate, rank, and relish in the pizza choice that pleases us most."

However, superimposing this example onto the marriage arena precipitates disastrous results!

"I surmise that over 50% of readers have met a minimum of 5 different types of people. Hair texture, eye color, shape, and genetics contribute to the varieties our personalities have experienced. Because of this vast array, we have the "**MIS**fortune" of being able to rate, rank, and relish in the human choice that pleases us most.

Husbands

A man who takes part in adultery has no sense; he will destroy himself. (Proverbs 6:32 NCV).

Do not desire her beauty in your heart, and do not let her capture you with her eyelashes; (Proverbs 6:25 ESV).

Chapter 9: Marriage

"I made an agreement with my eyes not to look at a young woman in a way that would make me want her." (Job 31:1 ERV).

Wives

In the same way, let me say a word to the women. You should be subject to your husbands, so that if there should be some who disobey the word, they may be won, without a word, through the behaviour of their wives, as they notice you conducting yourselves with reverence and purity. The beauty you should strive for ought not to be the external sort – elaborate hair-dressing, gold trinkets, fine clothes! Rather, true beauty is the secret beauty of the heart, of a sincere, gentle and quiet spirit. That is very precious to God. (1 Peter 3:1-4 NTE).

Couples

Marriage is to be honored by all and the marriage bed kept undefiled, because God will judge the sexually immoral and adulterers. (Hebrews 13:4 CSB).

Singles

You say, "I am allowed to do anything"—but not everything is good for you. And even though "I am allowed to do anything," I must not become a slave to anything. You say, "Food was made for the stomach, and the stomach for food." (This is true, though someday God will do away with both of them.) But you can't say that our bodies were made for sexual immorality. They were made for the Lord, and the Lord cares about our bodies. And God will raise us from the dead by his power, just as he raised our Lord from the dead. Don't you realize that your bodies are actually parts of Christ? Should a man take his body, which is part of Christ, and join it to a prostitute? Never! And don't you realize that if a man joins himself to a prostitute, he becomes one body with her? For the Scriptures say, "The two are united into one." But the person who is joined to the Lord is one spirit with him. Run from sexual sin! No other sin so clearly affects the body as this one does. For sexual immorality is a sin against your own body. Don't you realize that your body is the temple of the Holy Spirit, who lives in you and was given to you by God? You do not belong to yourself, for God bought you with a high price. So you must honor God with your body. (1 Corinthians 6:12-20 NLT).

Oh, let me warn you, sisters in Jerusalem: Don't excite love, don't stir it up, until the time is ripe—and you're ready. (Song of Solomon 8:4 The Message).

Technically, there are many choices for the human being looking to satisfy his or her "***craving***" for just the right person. However, for the new creation (2 Corinthians 5:17) there is only one choice to satisfy his or her **"*contentment*"** for the just the right person chosen by God.

Marriage

To make marriage work you MUST take the exit door off its hinges and erect a brick wall 54 feet deep in its place that can NEVER be penetrated. Marriage requires audacious commitment and the relentless courage to be *willingly, sacrificially*, and safely *sequestered* in this once in a lifetime \pportunity. The framework from which to build the mental perspective and paradigm for marriage is one man, one woman, for one lifetime. Life is messy. All have sinned and fallen short of God's glorious ideal for living this Christian life (Romans 3:23). But, still, we MUST try!

I do not claim that I have already succeeded or have already become perfect. I keep striving to win the prize for which Christ Jesus has already won me to himself. Of course, my friends, I really do not think that I have already won it; the one thing I do, however, is to forget what is behind me and do my best to reach what is ahead. So I run straight toward the goal in order to win the prize, which is God's call through Christ Jesus to the life above. (Philippians 3:12-14 GNT).

Confession

I, <u>Demario Rollins</u>, have a messy life full of mistakes. Many, many, many, many mistakes. But, I press on. Each day I'm given begins with a blank sheet of paper. I can choose how I want to write today's story through my thoughts, words, and actions. Today doesn't have to look like yesterday. You, dear reader, also may have a messy life full of mistakes. I encourage you to press on. Each day God chooses to wake you up is a day you've never seen before and a day you'll never see again. You can choose how you want to write today's story through your thoughts, words, and actions. Today doesn't have to look like yesterday.

If we confess our sins, he is faithful and righteous to forgive us our sins and to cleanse us from all unrighteousness. (1 John 1:9 CSB).

Prayer

Heavenly Father, forgive us for entering the sacred covenant of marriage and not giving it the exclusive commitment in heart, mind, and soul it deserves. Marriage is Your conception and therefore should be done Your way. Fill us with Your Holy Spirit so that we will be enabled to love our spouses unconditionally as we endeavor to have earthly marriages that reflect the relationship between Christ and the Church.

Chapter 9: Marriage

Love

I am fairly certain that spouses don't wake up in the morning with malevolent intentions to cause mental, emotional, or spiritual harm to the pulchritudinous life partner who they have vowed to love. Building on this perspective, I humbly interject these 2 strategies into the quest for peace in the marital relationship.

Strategy #1: We only have one Enemy.

For we are not struggling against human beings, but against the rulers, authorities and cosmic powers governing this darkness, against the spiritual forces of evil in the heavenly realm. (Ephesians 6:12 CJB).

It is my pleasure to tell you emphatically and with the certainty of God's Holy Word that your spouse is NOT your enemy.

From that time, Jesus began to show his disciples that he had to go to Jerusalem and suffer many things from the elders, chief priests, and experts in the law, and be killed, and on the third day be raised again. Peter took him aside and began to rebuke him, saying, "May you receive mercy, Lord! This will never happen to you." But Jesus turned and said to Peter, "Get behind me, Satan! You are a snare to me because you are not thinking the things of God, but the things of men." (Matthew 16:21-23 EHV).

Peter had *good intentions*. Peter was *concerned*. Peter was a *close friend*. Peter was *protective*. But, lamentably and unknowingly, Peter was being used by Satan. Inevitably I'm going to be wrong about <u>one couple</u> reading this section but I'm going to proceed anyway. I believe that your spouse has good *intentions.* I believe that your spouse is *concerned* about you. I believe that your spouse is a *close friend* and is very *protective* of you. But, lamentably and unknowingly, your spouse is susceptible to being used by Satan. We all are. Therefore, It is my pleasure to tell you emphatically and with the certainty of God's Holy Word that your spouse is NOT your enemy. Let forgiveness, peace, harmony, and unconditional love be permanent residents in your heart, home, and marriage.

"Through prayer, make sure we're fighting the one true adversary
   who seeks our destruction, Satan."

Strategy #2: "You know my heart."

> *But from the beginning of the creation, God 'made them male and female.' 'For this reason a man shall leave his father and mother and be joined to his wife, and the two shall become one flesh'; so then they are no longer two, but one flesh. Therefore what God has joined*

Chapter 9: Marriage

together, let not man separate." (Mark 10:6-9 NKJV).

Husbands and wives are joined together in multiple ways that are both obvious to senses and elusive to comprehension. A very special bond couples share is love from one heart to another. When our spouses say or do something that we perceive to be mean, offensive, hurtful, inappropriate, impolite, or disrespectful...I challenge you to *pause*, take a deep breath and think about his/her heart for 22 seconds. Inevitably I'm going to be wrong about <u>one more couple</u> reading this section but I'm going to proceed anyway.

Your spouse:

1. Likes you.
2. Chose you.
3. Touches you.
4. Supports you.
5. Respects you.
6. Listens to you.
7. Flirts with you.
8. Prays for you.
9. Prioritizes you.
10. Laughs with you.
11. Sacrifices for you.
12. Compliments you.
13. Is your best friend.
14. Is in love with you.

15. Is interested in you.
16. Is excited about you.
17. Was and is attracted to you.
18. Misses you when you're gone.
19. Values spending time with you.
20. Works very hard for your family.
21. Verbally builds you up in your absence.
22. Thought enough of you to permanently cancel all other options for companionship and commit to be with you exclusively for life.

(If you are the *one more couple* that this list doesn't describe, you're welcome to use it as a reference for areas to work on in your marriage).

While you paused for 22 seconds to think about your spouse's heart, I prepared these 22 characteristics of **your** spouse and I have good news to report! They don't seem to be synonymous with being mean, offensive, hurtful, inappropriate, impolite, or disrespectful. Therefore, my conclusion is that you have simply "misunderstood" your sweetheart. Let forgiveness, peace, harmony, and unconditional love be permanent residents in your heart, home, and marriage.

"Through prayer, make sure we're fighting the one true adversary who seeks our destruction, Satan."

> *Love is patient, love is kind. It does not envy, it does not boast, it is not proud. It does not dishonor others, it is not self-seeking, it is not easily angered, it*

Chapter 9: Marriage

keeps no record of wrongs. Love does not delight in evil but rejoices with the truth. It always protects, always trusts, always hopes, always perseveres. Love never fails. (1 Corinthians 13:4-8a NIV).

And now these three remain: faith, hope and love. But the greatest of these is love. (1 Corinthians 13:13 NIV).

Communication

Always remember that the words you say, how you say them, when you say them, and the expression you use while communicating play a vital role in your transmission being received appropriately with love and grace. **Timing. Words. Tone. Expression.**

Remember this, my dear friends! Everyone must be quick to listen, but slow to speak and slow to become angry. (James 1:19 GNT).

A Godly Marriage

But I want you to understand this: The head of every man is Christ, the head of a woman is the man, and the head of Christ is God. (1 Corinthians 11:3 NCV).

The institution of marriage, designed by God, is a reflection of Christ and the Church. Jesus Christ surrendered to the will of the **Father** in the plan of salvation (Luke 22:42). Both the man and the woman are commanded to be filled with the **Holy Spirit** (Ephesians 5:18) in submission to **Jesus Christ.** The man, filled with the Spirit and following the Savior, endeavors to live a life that allows the Son of God to continue His work through the man. His thoughts, actions, and speech should reflect a life surrendered to his first love (Revelation 2:4). When the man is aligned with the will of God and in step with the Spirit (Galatians 5:25), he is then positioned to be the head of a life partner who is commanded to submit (Ephesians 5:22) to him. The beautiful picture looks like this:

A husband who submits to Christ + A wife who submits to her husband
= A Godly Marriage

The God I Know

*<u>Wants each man to **love** his wife as he loves himself and for the wife to **respect** her husband.</u>*
Husbands, go all out in your love for your wives, exactly as Christ did for the church—a love marked by giving, not getting. Christ's love makes the church whole. His words evoke her beauty. Everything he does and says is designed to bring the best out of her, dressing her in dazzling white silk, radiant with holiness.

Chapter 9: Marriage

And that is how husbands ought to love their wives. They're really doing themselves a favor—since they're already "one" in marriage. (Ephesians 5:25-28 MSG).

However, each man among you [without exception] is to love his wife as his very own self [with behavior worthy of respect and esteem, always seeking the best for her with an attitude of lovingkindness], and the wife [must see to it] that she respects and delights in her husband [that she notices him and prefers him and treats him with loving concern, treasuring him, honoring him, and holding him dear]. (Ephesians 5:33 Amplified Bible).

Chapter 10: Discipleship

"As humans, we are bent toward forgetting unless we are intentional." — Heather D. Rollins

In this chapter I want to share an intense 4 week discipleship experience that I put together as one of the by-products of the story "Fan the Flame" from the fifth chapter.

First, you need to find a small group of same gender friends who would be willing to go on this journey with you. The first four weeks are packed with many features that will help determine how committed your group is to one another and to growing in the Lord.

The purpose of a discipleship group like this would be to enrich and encourage the spiritual life of others so that they can do the same. Life is busy. Very busy. But, as Heather D. Rollins would say, "As humans, we are bent toward forgetting unless we are intentional".

If we are not intentional, there is no way we can live like a people worthy of the call we have received as Ephesians 4:1 says.

We need to ensure that we are growing each day into the man or woman that God has called us to be. Indeed, He has chosen us and wishes to conform us to the image of His Son. This process of sanctification doesn't happen overnight and doesn't happen without our participation and intentionality. Having three or four other souls to hold us accountable fosters suitable grounds in the quest to succeed at becoming more like Jesus. I had never started or participated in a discipleship group so I just let my imagination roam free as I awaited direction from the Holy Spirit. What I will present below is the format that emanated.

First I thought, I should probably try to get to know these guys. So, I created 30 questions. I decided to ask one question each day. The first 15 questions were general and the last 15 questions went deeper as to reveal key aspects of their walk with God. The answers to the first 15 questions would help me to relate to them and the final 15 questions would provide enough information to design lessons with topics that would be relevant to where they were on their journey with the Creator.

Discipleship Group Questions

1. How can I pray for you?

Chapter 10: Discipleship

2. What is your birthday?
3. Where were you born (city/state)?
4. What is your favorite food? ****SPIRITUAL GIFT ASSESSMENT****
5. What is your favorite restaurant in Searcy? ****GROUP ME****
6. What is your favorite sport to play?
7. What is your favorite sport to watch?
8. What is your favorite card game?
9. What is your favorite board game? ****3:16PM ALARMS & PRAYER****
10. What 2 things do you consider yourself to be very good at?
11. What do you do for exercise?
12. What are your hobbies?
13. Do you have any hidden talents? What are they? ****GRATITUDE LIST****
14. What do you do for a living?
15. How many children do you have? What are their names and ages? ****CashApp, Venmo, ApplePay****
16. What is your favorite Bible verse?
17. What translation of the Bible do you like best?
18. How would you spend your time for Jesus if you didn't have to work? ****RECAP****
19. What is your greatest obstacle in sharing the gospel with others?
20. What topical study from the Bible interests you personally? ****THE LIST****

21. What unanswered questions do you have about God's Word?
22. Do you know what your spiritual gift is or what your spiritual gifts are? (Romans 12:6-8, 1 Corinthians 12:4-11, Ephesians 4:11-13, 1 Peter 4:10-11) Answer Yes or No.
23. Do you have a mission statement for your life?
24. Do you know your purpose?
25. Is there a sin in your life that is recurrent and consistently defeats you?

Answer Yes or No. ****SEND CASH FOR WEEK 4****

26. What biblical discipline(s) give(s) you the most spiritual satisfaction?
27. From which bible story are you able to make the most application to your life? ****S.M.O.A.S.****
28. How do you personally "practice the presence" of God in your own life?
29. Do you look forward to Judgement Day or are you fearful of it ?
30. What legacy do you want to leave on Earth once you're in Heaven with Jesus?

Ask the initial 4 questions as direct messages to your group members; perhaps through text message or phone call. Prior to reaching question **5**, create a GroupMe (or similar) account and invite all of them to join. It is important to choose a theme verse for your group and name the chat forum accordingly so that intentionality remains front and center. For example, if

Chapter 10: Discipleship

you use Philippians 3:13-14 as a theme you could name your group " Pressing Toward the Mark".

Brethren, I count not myself to have apprehended: but this one thing I do, forgetting those things which are behind, and reaching forth unto those things which are before, I press toward the mark for the prize of the high calling of God in Christ Jesus. (Philippians 3:13-14 KJV).

Start your group on a Sunday. Make a habit of asking each member how you can pray for them for that particular week. Keep a prayer journal of names, dates, prayer requests, and be sure to document the answers God will surely give in the coming weeks.

After asking question **4**, send this message:

Spiritual Gifts (Week 1 Project)

I'd like to know how God has gifted you. Please take this survey at your leisure. Set a goal to complete it within 7 days (at this juncture you would provide a link to a spiritual gifts assessment questionnaire; there are many choices on the internet)

After asking question **9**, send this message:

3:16 Begins

Let's pray for one another! As you know, John 3:16 is a very special scripture in the Holy Bible. In honor of that scripture, let's set an alarm on our phones for

3:16 PM. At that time we will take a moment to pray , even if it's only 7 seconds (because our lives are very demanding!) At 3:16pm, remember the names of our group members and ask God to help them with their petitions.

After asking question **13**, send this message:

Gratitude (Week 2 Project)

It's been really great getting to know you over the past 14 days! Our first weekly assignment was to take the spiritual gifts assessment. Next we're going to create gratitude lists. Over the next 7 days think about some things you're grateful for. Between 10 and 20 items will be sufficient.

After asking question **15**, it's time to determine the easiest way to send your group members a small portion of money. Consider setting aside $2 to $10 per group member for a future project called *S.M.O.A.S.* — send this message:

CashApp, Venmo, ApplePay?

What's the best way to send you money for a future group project?

After asking question **18**, send a Recap to the group:

Chapter 10: Discipleship

Recap

    List your group title with acronym
    List your group start date
    List your GroupMe (or similar) start date
    List weekly projects (week 1,2 and 3 upcoming)
    After asking question **20**, send this message:

The List (Week 3 Project)

I appreciate the effort you have put forth over the past two weeks in:

1. Taking a spiritual gifts assessment.
2. Creating a gratitude list.

This week we're going to focus on "The List". This is a list of 5 activities you feel like you "should" be doing in your "personal" quest to be a disciple of Jesus Christ. As an example, review Demario's list below. The activities you list are personal nudges you get on the inside from the Holy Spirit as He encourages you to follow Jesus.

1. Witness to the lost.
2. Disciple a believer.
3. Teach God's Word.
4. Give generously.
5. Prayer with the Almighty.

After asking question **25**, send money to each group member through the platform of their choosing.

After asking question **27**, send this message:

S.M.O.A.S. (Week 4 Project)

I appreciate the effort you have put forth over the past three weeks in:

1. Taking a spiritual gifts assessment.
2. Creating a gratitude list.
3. Creating "The List" of five.

This week we're going to take the **S.M.O.A.S.** challenge. By now you all should have received money via CashAPP, ApplePay or Venmo (or whatever platform they chose). Your mission over the next 7 days is to find an opportunity to **S**pend **M**oney **O**n **A S**tranger. The best scenario is to personally present this money to someone you have never met, perhaps at a grocery store or gas station. When the person asks why you would do such a thing, you respond: "***All that I have belongs to Jesus Christ and He placed it on my heart to share this with you. How can I pray for you or your family today***?" If more needs to be said, the Holy Spirit will guide your thoughts and words. I look forward to hearing the wonderful works of our Savior through His faithful disciple who is pressing toward the mark (Philippians 3:14)!

Chapter 10: Discipleship

> *But do not forget to do good and to share, for with such sacrifices God is well pleased.* (Hebrews 13:16 NKJV).

Then you would conclude the month with the final 3 questions over the next 3 days:
28. How do you personally "practice the presence" of God in your own life?
29. Do you look forward to Judgement Day or are you fearful of it?
30. What legacy do you want to leave on Earth once you're in Heaven with Jesus?

Scripture References for the Discipleship Group components

Weekly prayer requests: *Therefore, confess your sins to one another, and pray for one another so that you may be healed. A prayer of a righteous person, when it is brought about, can accomplish much.* (James 5:16 NASB).

Spiritual Gift Assessment (Week 1): *We all have different gifts. Each gift came because of the grace that God gave us. If one has the gift of prophecy, he should use that gift with the faith he has.* (Romans 12:6 ICB).

3:16 begins: Pray regularly. (1 Thessalonians 5:17 CJB).

Gratitude List (Week 2): *in every situation [no matter what the circumstances] be thankful and continually give thanks to God; for this is the will of*

God for you in Christ Jesus. (1 Thessalonians 5:18 Amplified Bible).

The List (Week 3**)**: *Use your time well, for these are evil days.* (Ephesians 5:16 CJB).

S.M.O.A.S. (Week 4): *Share with God's people who need help.* (Romans 12:13a).

What I have outlined is simply a template. Adjust, modify, add, and subtract as you see fit. The purpose is to create an environment where established Christians can be accountable to one another for being "doers" of the Word.

"As humans, we are bent toward forgetting unless we are intentional" — Heather D. Rollins

The God I Know

<u>*Has given us a Great Commission*</u> and He intends for us to live in obedience to the plan He has given us to follow.

> *Go therefore and make disciples of all the nations [help the people to learn of Me, believe in Me, and obey My words], baptizing them in the name of the Father and of the Son and of the Holy Spirit, teaching them to observe everything that I have commanded you; and lo, I am with you always [remaining*

Chapter 10: Discipleship

with you perpetually—regardless of circumstance, and on every occasion], even to the end of the age." (Matthew 28:19-20 Amplified Bible).

Bonus Material: "If I Should Fall Away"

What you are about to read is my response to a question that was asked of me. Here's the question:

"Demario, I have a friend who used to be committed to Christ and the Church but it seems that she has fallen away. What advice do you have on how I should approach her? I'm concerned about her salvation and really want her to be in Heaven with us.

Start with prayer! God blesses the effort of rescue missions.

My dear friends, if you know people who have wandered off from God's truth, don't write them off. Go after them. Get them back and you will have rescued precious lives from destruction and prevented an epidemic of wandering away from God. (James 5:20 The Message).

People fall into one of two categories. Saved or Lost. There is no in-between. Those who have "fallen away" were perhaps never truly "born again."

They left us. However, they were never really part of us. If they had been, they would have stayed with us. But by leaving they made it clear that none of them were part of us. (1 John 2:19 NOG).

Those who have been _truly born again_ are new creations. (2 Corinthians 5:17).

They have been given God's Spirit (1 John 4:13) and have been sealed (Ephesians 1:13). The miracle and beauty of being **_truly born again_** is that the "*relationship*" remains even when the "*fellowship*" is broken. An example of this is the prodigal son (Luke 15:11-32). Though he severed the "*fellowship*" he enjoyed with his father, he did not and could not sever the "*relationship*". Though his actions were contrary to the will of his father, they were incapable of terminating the truth of the father-son relationship. When the son repented, he was welcomed with open arms.

God _still_ hates sin...equally so, He _still_ loves the sinner.

"Now, if evil people change their lives, they will live and not die. They might stop doing all the bad things

Chapter 10: Discipleship

they did and begin to carefully obey all my laws. They might become fair and good. God will not remember all the bad things they did. He will remember only their goodness, so they will live!" The Lord God says, "I don't want evil people to die. I want them to change their lives so that they can live! (Ezekial 18:21-23 ERV).

God is withholding the return of Jesus to give His "_creation_" time to accept the invitation to become "_children_".

The Lord is not slack concerning his promise, as some men count slackness; but is longsuffering to us-ward, not willing that any should perish, but that all should come to repentance. (2 Peter 3:9 KJV).

Here are 7 helpful devotionals from my book called "_Destination Heartland: 183 Devotionals to Plant in 365 days._"

Scripture for today (#42): You didn't choose me. I chose you. (John 15:16a NLT)
Application for today: You are important. You are special. You are necessary. You are not an accident. Almighty God chose you!

Scripture for today (#43): For I am confident of this very thing, that He who began a good work in you will perfect it until the day of Christ Jesus. (Philippians 1:6 NASB)

Application for today: Today you may feel like you have an "Under Construction" sign on the billboard of your life. You're not alone. We are all "works in progress" and Jesus will continue His work until He calls us home. He's not finished with you yet!

Scripture for today (#48): For the time being no discipline brings joy, but seems sad *and* painful; yet to those who have been trained by it, afterwards it yields the peaceful fruit of righteousness [right standing with God and a lifestyle and attitude that seeks conformity to God's will and purpose]. (Hebrews 12:11 Amplified Bible)

Application for today: My dear child, don't shrug off God's discipline, but don't be crushed by it either. It's the child he loves that he disciplines; the child he embraces, he also corrects. God is educating you; that's why you must never drop out. He's treating you as dear children. This trouble you're in isn't punishment; it's *training*, the normal experience of children. (Hebrews 12:5-7 The Message)

Chapter 10: Discipleship

Scriptures for today (#50):
Jeremiah 31:34b (NLT): "And I will forgive their wickedness, and I will never again remember their sins."

Hebrews 8:12b (NLT): "And I will forgive their wickedness, and I will never again remember their sins."

Hebrews 10:17b (NLT): "I will never again remember their sins and lawless deeds."

Application for today: When a teacher "purposely" repeats something in school, it will most likely be on the test. When God repeats something 3 times, He must REALLY mean it!

Then Jesus stood up again and said to the woman, "Where are your accusers? Didn't even one of them condemn you?" "No, Lord," she said. And Jesus said, "Neither do I. Go and sin no more." (John 8:10-11 NLT)

Scripture for today (#63): God destined us to be his adopted children through Jesus Christ because of his love. This was according to his goodwill and plan (Ephesians 1:5 CEB)

Application for today: You may be confused, puzzled, worried, perplexed and anxious about the future. Listen very closely...God ALWAYS has a **plan**!

Your eyes saw me when I was still an unborn child. Every day of my life was recorded in your book before one of them had taken place. (Psalm 139:16 God's Word Translation)

The God I Know

Go ahead and make all the plans you want, but it's the Lord who will ultimately direct your steps. (Proverbs 16:1 The Passion Translation)

Scriptures for today (#65): Humans can reproduce only human life, but the Holy Spirit gives birth to spiritual life. So don't be surprised when I say, 'You must be born again.' (John 3:6-7 NLT) The wind blows where it wishes and you hear its sound, but you do not know where it is coming from and where it is going; so it is with everyone who is born of the Spirit. (John 3:8 AMP)

Application for today: Spiritual birth is an intangible process performed from start to finish by the Trinity. Let's be careful "*not to judge*" (in a condemning way) whether this miraculous experience has or has not occurred in someone else's life. The conversion process is precious and personal between each created soul and the Creator. If we have doubts about someone else's salvation, we should encourage and pray for that individual daily and "expect" to see positive fruit in their life.

Scriptures for today (#68): And the man said to me, "Daniel, *you are very precious to God*, so listen carefully to what I have to say to you (Daniel 10:11a NLT)

Chapter 10: Discipleship

"Don't be afraid," he said, "***for you are very precious to God***. Peace! Be encouraged! Be strong!" As he spoke these words to me, I suddenly felt stronger and said to him, "Please speak to me, my lord, for you have strengthened me." (Daniel 10:19 NLT)

For ***God does not show favoritism***. (Romans 2:11 NLT)

Then Peter replied, "I see very clearly that ***God shows no favoritism***. (Acts 10:34 NLT)

Application for today: Daniel 10:19 + Romans 2:11 = **You** are very precious to God!!!!!

(Note: **bold** and *italics* added for emphasis)

Summary:

1. Pray, pray, pray!
2. Show more interest in befriending her than in saving her.

I planted, Apollos watered, but God gave the growth. So neither the one who plants nor the one who waters is anything, but only God who gives the growth. The one who plants and the one who waters have a common purpose, and each will receive wages according to the labor of each. (1 Corinthians 3:6-8 NRSV).

3. Take time to listen and find out where she is spiritually.
4. Show unconditional love for and toward her and establish trust.
5. Trust will open the door for you to share "your story" and evidence of God's goodness and grace found all around us. Gently incorporate thoughts, topics, and evidence of God into regular conversation.
6. Through prayer, interest, love, and conversation…perhaps her heart will change from stone to flesh (Ezekial 36:26; Acts 16:14)
7. Practice the "Ministry of Reconciliation" daily (2 Corinthians 5:11-21)

The God I Know

<u>Loved the world so much that He gave His one and only Son</u> so that whoever believes in Him may not be lost, but have eternal life. God did not send his Son into the world to judge the world guilty, but to save the world through him. (John 3:16-17 NCV).

And that's about it, friends. Be cheerful. Keep things in good repair. Keep your spirits up. Think in harmony. Be agreeable. Do all that, and the God of love and

Chapter 10: Discipleship

peace will be with you for sure. Greet one another with a holy embrace. All the brothers and sisters here say hello. The amazing grace of the Master, Jesus Christ, the extravagant love of God, the intimate friendship of the Holy Spirit, be with all of you. (2 Corinthians 13:11-14 The Message).

I close my letter with these last words: Be happy. Grow in Christ. Pay attention to what I have said. Live in harmony and peace. And may the God of love and peace be with you. Greet each other warmly in the Lord. All the Christians here send you their best regards. May the grace of our Lord Jesus Christ be with you all. May God's love and the Holy Spirit's friendship be yours. (2 Corinthians 13:11-14 The Living Bible).

Endnotes

1 Dictionary.com Online, s.v. "lonely," accessed February 9, 2021, https://www.dictionary.com/browse/lonely?s=

2 Dictionary.com Online, s.v. "purpose," accessed February 9, 2021, https://www.dictionary.com/browse/purpose?s=t